GOVERNMENT CREEP
What the Government is Doing
That You Don't Know About

For Greg Piccionelli
with Thanks for all
you do for our freedom.

by *Philip D. Harvey*

Phil Harvey

Loompanics Unlimited
Port Townsend, Washington

Government Creep
What the Government is Doing That You Don't Know About
© 2003 by Philip D. Harvey

Published by:
Loompanics Unlimited
PO Box 1197
Port Townsend, WA 98368
Loompanics Unlimited is a division of Loompanics Enterprises, Inc.
Phone: 360-385-2230
E-mail: service@loompanics.com
Web site: www.loompanics.com

Cover art by Craig Howell, Cheeba Productions

ISBN 1-55950-234-7
Library of Congress Card Catalog Number 2003102495

Contents

About the Author

Philip D. Harvey is president of DKT International, a non-profit family planning and AIDS prevention organization, and president and majority shareholder of Adam & Eve, a mail order business that sells sexually oriented books and films.

President Jimmy Carter praised his first book, *Let Every Child Be Wanted*, as a "lively and interesting" contribution to our understanding of foreign aid programs.

His second, *The Government vs. Erotica*, tells the story of his own small company's victory over the Justice Department after an eight-year battle.

Here's what the critics said.

"A frightening, enlightening story." — Media Coalition

"A powerful indictment of those who would force their narrow view of the world on a free people." — *Caspar Star Tribune*

"An excellent anecdotal way to get a handle on the ongoing pornography debate." —*Publishers Weekly*

"Readers concerned about free speech will enjoy this surprisingly involving tale." — *Booklist*

"A clear and concise look into the inner workings of a modern day persecution... A significant chronicle in the evolution of First Amendment political debate." — *Wisconsin Lawyer*

INTRODUCTION
Very Personal Problems

The greater dangers to liberty lurk in insidious encroachment by men of zeal, well meaning but without understanding. — Justice Louis Brandeis

Tell everyone you meet that our huge federal government can exert power over their lives and you'll find that most, if not all, will agree. But very few people realize how much power today's government has over private citizens and how tyrannically it can — and does — exercise that power.

We're not as alert to the danger as we might be because Big Brother tendencies usually seem so abstract. This book is designed to make them personal and vivid. It presents seventeen stories that typify the devastating impact of an ever-bigger government on millions of ordinary Americans. While the stories' characters and locations are fictitious, they describe events that have occurred and are occurring regularly, as you will see from the sections titled "What's Happening Here."

Today the need to be on our guard is stronger than ever, since the Bush administration assumed vast new powers in 2001/2002 to detain people without charging them with a crime and to incarcerate anyone perceived to be an alleged dangerous "enemy combatant." Such steps have been taken before in wartime, but the "war" against organized terrorism will likely go on indefinitely. Sweeping wartime powers must not. Remember, you too could be considered an "enemy combatant" by an overzealous government.

As it creeps slowly, unnoticeably into our lives, our government taps the phones of people who are not under suspicion; takes taxes from middle-income wage earners to pay huge subsidies to wealthy farmers, creates pointless hurdles for small businesses, routinely attacks and censors our entertainment and our reading for its sexual content, and seizes hundreds of millions of dollars in property from people who are not even accused of crimes.

Our constitutional right to due process, significantly weakened before 9/11, is now being deeply undermined. Our right to privacy on the Internet is being threatened by a government grab for a monopoly on coding information. At airports, thousands of Americans have been strip-searched, not for dangerous weapons but on mere suspicion of possessing drugs that pose no immediate threat. And our police and judicial systems continue to be corrupted and undermined by the "war on drugs."

It almost seems as if we Americans are willing to give up our rights. Let's throw the drug dealers in jail! (Surely suspicion won't fall on anyone in my family.) Let's stop offensive, violent, sexual TV. (Surely the good ideas won't be suppressed along with the bad.) Let's tap the phones of offenders, and confiscate their property without a trial, and search them if we think they're dangerous. (Such a thing could never happen to me!) These assumptions are not uncommon: In a recent survey nearly half of all Americans said they think the First Amendment goes too far, protects too many rights.

Beware. The erosion of our freedoms continues; gradually, cumulatively, and extensively. Too many people have gone to jail; too many people have lost their homes, their cars, their boats, and their cash; too many people have been harassed, their vehicles stopped, their persons searched, merely because they fit a "profile" of someone the government thought might be misbehaving.

The government does all this by force. It takes our money, taps our phones, tells us what to read and say, removes our property, dictates our sexual behavior, decides on the skin color of the children we may adopt, deprives us of the right to earn a living — all for our own good, to promote our own happiness, and to create "order."

But for the most part, order comes naturally to human societies. Just look at the orderliness of voluntary economic activity, the remarkably complex systems that stock the shelves of our supermarkets, for example. Left alone, we are generally very good at organizing our families, our communities, and our economic lives. Yet given money and power (and we have given our government lots of both), politicians and bureaucrats seem inexorably driven to make more "rules" for all of us.

We pay for our own disempowerment. We pay the taxes that enable the government to keep creeping into our lives. Our money is taken in such vast amounts that we can no longer grasp its dimensions. The government's annual cut of our earnings is now $1.8 *trillion* — $1,800,000,000,000 — a few thousand from you, a few thousand from me, and a few thousand from a hundred million others. This gives the federal government almost inconceivable power.

On top of spending our money to undermine our liberties, the government also wastes it. It uses our taxes to subsidize the advertising of raisins in Japan, to further enrich a group of multimillionaire sugar growers in Florida, to provide economic favors to politically nimble but otherwise corrupt companies.

Liberals and conservatives have joined hands in this quiet conspiracy. Liberals have always been comfortable interfering in the marketplace, telling us that we can or cannot work for certain wages, or do certain "licensed" tasks, or work under certain conditions that we may find agreeable but the government does not. Conservatives have always been comfortable dictating to us how we should behave in our private and sexual lives. "Conservatives want to be your daddy, telling you what to do and what not to do," states David Boaz, vice president of the Cato Institute in Washington, D.C. "Liberals want to be your mommy, feeding you, tucking you in, and wiping your nose."

Americans do not need a governmental parent. We'd rather be free. We'd rather be left alone to make a living, to form or work in community associations, to worship, or not, as we please, to read and write what we wish, to raise our children and send them to whatever schools we choose. These are not extreme desires. Indeed they match quite well the ideas embodied in the phrase "life, liberty, and the pursuit of happiness." But government creep threatens these values more and more every day, as you'll see when you read on.

I have witnessed some of the episodes in this book firsthand and researched the others in considerable detail. I have myself been indicted and tried on obscenity charges (and found not guilty by a jury after five minutes of deliberation). For twenty-five years, I have run a small business that requires dealing on a daily basis with the maze of government regulations — from the shape of toilet seats in our men's rooms to the conflicting requirements of nondiscrimination and sexual harassment laws. And I have run a nonprofit organization partly funded by government grants and seen firsthand how little the government cares about saving money. Indeed, once money is appropriated, the government is almost obsessive about spending it — never mind the waste.

Because government creeps, we tend to believe that the strip searches, the confiscation of property, the incarcerations will always happen to someone else. But because they are happening more and more to "people like us," we must stand up to government creep if we are to maintain our freedom.

CHAPTER ONE
Killing Anita's Business

Anita had decided to open her cheese shop. She was nervous about it because she did not really believe that she and her husband, Robert, could afford the financial risk, not quite yet, but she was forty years old, and opening her own cheese shop was her life's dream. At forty, she told herself, life was not a dress rehearsal. If she was going to do it, she had better do it now.

First there was the money. She had saved $10,000 from her doorman's job, and her grandfather's stock gift was now worth $14,000. Her sister had lent her $10,000 without interest and Robert had agreed to lend her $10,000 "at prime plus one." Her friend Diane had been outraged by this. "What kind of a husband would charge his wife interest on a loan?" she had asked, aghast.

But Anita thought that maybe he had a point. It was a business deal, after all. He wasn't getting any share of the profits if her cheese shop made money, so maybe he was right. She did wonder about the "plus one." Maybe just a flat rate of interest at today's prime would have sufficed. But Robert was something of a fussbudget and knew that prime plus one was a very good rate for a high-risk loan for a new business.

Robert did not mind being thought of as a fussbudget. When Anita was annoyed with something he'd been especially picky about, she often called him that, and he replied, "I like to keep things under control. I enjoy looking after details."

So she had $44,000, just about enough. She found a location and spent three months negotiating the terms of the lease with the landlady, Mrs. Singer. The landlady was happy to have a cheese shop on her premises, which was a good retail location on Second Avenue with twenty-five feet of frontage on the sidewalk, but she was annoyingly insistent on knowing lots of details, from what the store would offer (Would she sell Monterey Jack? Mrs. Singer loved Monterey Jack!), to whether or not she planned to hire "colored people." Anita reminded her that it would be illegal to hire or not to hire people on the basis of their skin color, but she didn't think that was really what mattered to Mrs. Singer. What Mrs. Singer wanted was to know the inside scoop. Anita did her best to oblige.

The work and the many steps required to open the shop were fraught with error, cost overruns, minor accidents, and, most of all, emotional strain. The subcontractor handling the demolition of the closets and dressing rooms of the previous women's clothing store had done his work in two days and departed leaving a horrible mess. The prime contractor claimed he couldn't start for three more weeks due to an emergency "prior" engagement. The cheese wholesaler had made it clear that he didn't take her business seriously, in no small part because she was a woman, and she was seething because that particular wholesaler carried several specialized cheeses she couldn't get anywhere else. She wanted to poke his eyes out.

And then there were the permits. Endless paperwork to be allowed to sell someone a slice of cheese. Cheese and other foods she expected to sell were for human consumption. That meant health authorities and inspections, and regulations for sink size and toilets and toilet seats and soap dishes. She needed a license to do business, registration with the tax authorities, and garbage collection. She was *told* who would pick up her garbage and at what price. No choice, no competition. It was like dealing with the Mafia, or so it seemed.

Robert, to his credit, was steadfastly supportive. With his "prime plus one" settled, he enthusiastically got behind "Cheese Plus One," which he agreed was a good name for the new store even though he knew it was a dig at him.

Finally the big day came. Cheese Plus One was open. Anita, her sister, Robert, and Diane all stood behind the counter, smiling as the first customers looked over the jarlsburgs and bries and cheddars. Business was brisk. Anita quickly learned which cheeses and breads would sell and how to get them replenished fast. There was an immediate demand for cold sodas which Anita resisted for several weeks, but she finally capitulated. If people were going to buy cheeses, breads, and salads for lunch they wanted their fruit-flavored ades and their diet Cokes and their raspberry-flavored seltzer water, so she grudgingly provided it. She had not intended to open a "soda" store.

For the first full year, Anita figured she lost money, although not much. Her accounts consisted of checkbook stubs and what went in and out of the cash register and not much else, but she did know whether the cash was coming up surplus or negative, and for many months it came up negative. In the second year it turned slightly positive, but it looked like a very long way to pay back the $20,000 of other people's money she had invested. In fact, based on the second year's profits, she calculated it would take three or four years to pay everybody back if she was going to pay herself even a modest salary.

On Wednesday and Saturday afternoons, a high school student named Dimitri came to the store to mop the floors and to clean the walk-in refrigerator. This took Dimitri about an hour. When he was done, Anita took five dollars out of the cash register and gave it to him. Robert, who worked for the New York Transit Authority, pointed out to her that this was an illegal transaction. He asked: "Could I persuade you to do this according to the rules?"

"You can argue with me to do this according to the rules 'til hell freezes over, but you know and I know there is no way I can possibly conform to all the rules when it comes to hiring somebody like Dimitri," she said. "Do you have any idea what I would have to go through?"

"Well, I know it doesn't make much sense for a small business like yours, but you could conceivably do it," said Robert.

"How could I conceivably do it? Instead of giving Dimitri $5 out of the cash register, I should sit down and fill out a FICA withholding form, take 35 cents out of his $5, stick it in an envelope, and send it to Washington, take another 35 cents out of my own pocket and send that to Washington, fill out umpteen forms, get on everybody's radar by having started with FICA, get the feds insisting that I withhold at least something for federal income tax even though he probably won't owe any, add state income tax forms and withholding, city income tax forms and withholding, are you kidding?"

"Well, you wouldn't have to do all that."

"Robert, you know that once Dimitri is registered as an employee with the Social Security people, the others are going to be all over me like flies on shit. They'll ruin me. I can't run this business that way. It's a borderline business; I may just make a little money this year, but not enough so that I even pay myself the minimum wage, but maybe just a little money. If I go through all that FICA stuff I don't have a prayer, I don't have a chance. Can't you see that? Don't you want your 'prime plus one'?"

"Okay, okay." In fact, Robert knew she was right. If she followed all the rules, she probably could not make any money, at least not at present sales levels.

In the third year, profits improved. Anita paid off her sister, who needed the money for other things, wrote herself a check for $2,000 at the end of every month, and declared to Robert: "I think I may just possibly make as much money doing this as I made as a doorman at the Wingate five years ago."

The health authorities had stopped by "Cheese Plus One" on several occasions, and had found a few minor violations. Anita had corrected these problems to the best of her ability as quickly as she could. But there were some ominous undertones from the regulators and inspectors. In addition to Dimitri, she paid one of her part-time clerks, Flora, "off the books" and she knew that they knew this. One of the New York State inspectors had told her very bluntly "off the record" that as long as she was just one small store, obviously not making very much money, she could probably get away with bending these rules, but if she wanted to expand her business, to open another store or two perhaps, she would be scrutinized very carefully. Her compliance with all federal, state, and city laws and regulations would be essential, and there would be no room for compromise.

Robert was not much help with this. Indeed, Robert, who had some legal training, was getting into his fussbudget mode. He was very uncomfortable with the whole arrangement. He felt duty bound to uphold the law. On the other hand, he was not about to rat on his own wife, so he decided that the best thing for him was just to be as uninformed about all these matters as possible. When it reached the point where he was uncomfortable even seeing Anita pay Dimitri or Flora from the cash register, he stopped coming by the store.

Anita spoke about these matters to her friend Ruben, who ran a successful restaurant near the garment district on Seventh Avenue. Ruben sneered at the employment regulations and the possibility of ever following them. "Of course you've got to have employees off the books. In food retailing, there's no alternative. If restaurants and stores like yours couldn't pay people to clean and do other work without going through all that government crap, there would be no food service retailing in this city. It's obvious. You've made the calculations. You have maybe the equivalent of two full-time employees besides yourself. In order to fully comply with all these regulations, you would have to hire an extra full-timer — and I mean that — a thirty-three percent increase in your payroll just to handle the paperwork. You can't do it. You can't afford it. I know that; the city knows that. I've been in the restaurant business for eighteen years. I've always paid most of my cleaning staff off the books. The city knows that if I couldn't pay them off the books I wouldn't be able to hire them and my restaurant would be less clean. So they look the other way. Government is for shmucks. As far as I'm concerned, its main purpose is to try to prevent people like you and me from making a living and from providing things that other people want. They can all go fuck themselves as far as I'm concerned."

Anita was not quite so sure. Before opening her store she had always believed in minimum wage laws and Social Security as something helpful to the poor. Now she realized that such requirements could also prevent you from hiring people who wanted to work. Indeed, in addition to the FICA Social Security payments which she was not withholding from Dimitri's salary (or paying on his behalf) she might even be violating minimum wage laws because he sometimes took more than one hour to do his clean-up. The fact that he got diverted flirting with Flora, a flamboyant and outspokenly sexual woman nearly three times his age, would not be recognized as a mitigating factor. If, with these diversions, it took him two hours to finish his clean-up, his pay was only $2.50 per hour, illegally low. On top of that, she thought he was probably only fifteen or sixteen years old — another law violated!

Cheese Plus One continued to serve an increasing and increasingly loyal clientele, and the business grew. Soon Anita was paying herself a salary of $50,000 a year and beginning to think about expanding. She was especially proud because Cheese Plus One seemed to have been a tipping point for a neighborhood in transition. As her business was growing, a gift shop opened down the block and the café across the avenue was spruced up, with new tables on the sidewalk and bright green and white umbrellas.

Anita sat down with a calculator and started running some numbers. She assumed that the dark threats from the state inspector were serious, that if she opened another store she would be scrutinized and forced to follow laws and regulations much more closely.

She asked for Robert's help with this, which he gladly gave. If his wife was "going straight" he was there! But he had to admit the figures just didn't add up. Even assuming that one person could handle the added paperwork for two shops, which they both thought would work, the increase in the burden for people like Dimitri added up very quickly. Instead of getting five dollars from the cash register on Wednesdays and Saturdays, Dimitri would have to get fifteen dollars a week (they recognized he wouldn't work for any less) which meant that his pay would probably have to be more than that to cover the deductions, and Anita would have to cover both employer and employee Social Security payments. That came to $2.30 a week times fifty-two weeks times two Dimitris, or $239 additional annual expense plus whatever increase might be needed to cover income tax withholding. The clerk accountant would cost an additional $20,000, plus benefits. She figured the net increase in the cost of clerical help for going "on the books" would come to about $5,000 per year, in part because it was harder to find people who were willing to work with all the official deductions and forms.

"I've got to figure what's in it for me," Anita said to Robert. "If I pay myself $50,000 a year and we assume that that goes on top of your salary of $61,000, then how much of that $50,000 do I get to keep?" They came up with some pretty gloomy projections. Federal income tax withholding on her salary would be $10,400; her personal Social Security burden would be $3,800; state and city income tax withholding would come to just under $4,000. In addition, she'd have to pay the employer's portion of the Social Security tax, another $3,800. Thus, the government take from her salary came to more than $22,000 and that did not count workmen's compensation, state disability payments, and federal and state unemployment insurance, all of which were mandatory. Altogether it looked like the deductions and payments would add up to half of her $50,000 salary.

"So I get to work eighty hours a week," said Anita. "I open up that store at ten o'clock in the morning and close it at ten o'clock at night, and I get to keep half of what I make?"

"That's the way it looks," said Robert. "There may be a way around the tax trap, but I'm not a tax lawyer and I can't see what it would be."

Anita decided not to open another store. All the cards seemed stacked against her.

In addition, some of the joy seemed to be seeping out of Cheese Plus One. Anita had been shaken by the discovery that she was violating so many laws and regulations with Dimitri and Flora. She did not like violating the law. Having decided not to open a new store, she calculated what it would cost her to comply with all laws and regulations in the existing store. The result, she found, would not leave her enough to be worth the continuing effort. In addition, Mrs. Singer was threatening a second increase in the rent when her lease came up for renewal. After five years, she decided to sell or close.

There were no takers for the business at a price that exceeded what she figured she could get on liquidation. So, six months later, the equipment and supplies were auctioned off.

The auction brought in $22,785, enough to pay Robert's prime-plus-one. Anita had thought she might cry to see her five-year dream sold off to the highest bidder, but she didn't. The refrigerators and the expensive Hobart meat slicer brought the most money; she was amused that even sheets of aluminum that had been used to protect the walls from grease spatters brought $1.50 each. Although she was reminded of those ads on TV where farmers' equipment is auctioned off and someone always sheds a tear, she thought, "They probably have other choices in life too. I certainly do. There are a lot of opportunities and a lot of jobs in America whether you've been a farmer or a cheese store owner. I'm sure I'll find one that I like. Too bad it couldn't have been this."

What's Happening Here

It is often the law of unintended consequences that makes government the enemy of progress. Minimum wage laws, Social Security payments, and income tax withholding all seem like parts of progressive, useful policies. But the unintended consequences of such policies can cripple employment opportunities for many of the people who need them most, strangle tiny new businesses before they've had a chance to succeed, and prevent new businesses from even getting started. It is well to remember that sixty percent of the jobs in America are with small companies. More than ninety percent of new jobs — the jobs that make it possible for young people to get started on a life of financial responsibility — are in businesses that employ fewer than 100 people. When government imposes unnecessary burdens on such businesses, government is a job-killer. When government regulations interfere with people's ability to do business with each other, to trade, to serve each other through commercial transactions, government is a part of the problem and not part of the solution.

The astonishing wealth created by the American economy over the past two centuries has been accomplished by free market capitalism. The United States has traditionally been a place where the government left people free to do business with each other and that environment is really the only one truly conducive to economic progress. A striking example of this is the remarkable success of the Chinese in Taiwan and in Hong Kong relative to the Chinese in China. In just fifty years since the Second World War, Taiwanese citizens — largely left free to do business among themselves and with the rest of the world — have created a nation with a per capita income of $13,000 per annum; the Hong Kong Chinese are even wealthier. Contrast that with the per capita GNP of about $300 for mainland China, where serious economic liberalization was instituted only a decade or so ago.

While the United States at one time tended to follow laissez-faire policies on economic matters, this is becoming less and less true. Since the Second World War especially, the U.S. government has imposed a growing battery of regulations and such regressive and job-killing taxes as the Social Security tax. The Social Security tax comes very close to being a tax on the poor to provide benefits to the rich; the tax must be paid on the first dollar earned by even the lowest income earners. The less educated, lower wage workers pay the tax for more years than their more educated counterparts because they start work earlier in life, often in their teens. Because their incomes are lower, the 7.65% Social Security and Medicare withholding tax, for which there are no exemptions whatsoever, is a larger portion of their total tax burden. Lower income people pay this tax on all of their income whereas those who make more than $87,000 a year pay no Social Security tax on any earnings over that amount. Furthermore, low-income people live less long than their wealthier brethren, and therefore collect fewer benefits at the end of life. Nobel Laureate economist Milton Friedman has correctly referred to the Social Security tax as "a regressive tax imposed at one of the worst places in the economic structure," with benefits taking the form of "a subsidy program in which the largest subsidies go to the people who have earned the highest incomes."

As the government confiscates more and more of our earnings and our wealth — government at all levels now consumes nearly thirty percent of our gross national product — it becomes even more difficult for businesses like Anita's to start and to succeed. Still, because the urge to do business is strong and because America continues to attract so many entrepreneur immigrants, thousands of new businesses do manage to get under way each year despite the regulations and the taxes. Sadly, many of those businesses, like Anita's friend Ruben's, flourish in defiance of the rules, leading to increasing contempt for the law and for the government.

The solution is relatively straightforward: lower taxes, fewer regulations.

CHAPTER TWO
"You're Not Entitled to a Lawyer"

Aziz stared at the hourglass-shaped splatter high on the cell wall where he had killed a cockroach with his shoe the week before. His shoes were rubberized slipper-like things they had issued him the day they locked him up. The shoes had no hard edges, no place to conceal anything, but they worked rather well for killing bugs.

Staring at the cockroach splatter the previous day, from the tiny bunk where he had spent seventy-four nights (or was it seventy-three?), Aziz had seen the wall start to rotate. He watched fascinated as the entire wall spun counter-clockwise, with the hourglass stain as the hub. He had been quite certain he was going mad.

Today the wall stayed in place, two vertical lines, two horizontal lines outlining the edges of the square of one wall of his solitary cubicle. There were numerous drips and stains on the gray-green paint but the cockroach dominated all the other marks in both size and clarity.

The hourglass shape reminded him of his wife, Tabitha. Tabitha was from Iraq. She was a Muslim. Once, not long after they had married, he had ordered a merry widow corset from Frederick's of Hollywood and after a lot of giggling and negotiating, he convinced his young wife to put it on. With her breasts pushing out over the top and her hips flared out below she had been overwhelmingly desirable to Aziz and they had made love four times in the next three days.

Tabitha was not inclined toward these excesses. She had a bright smile and a quick laugh, but she kept her head covered in public and, in the company of her brother, she regularly attended a nearby mosque, which was the largest one in Milwaukee.

Aziz was a lapsed Presbyterian. As a boy he had been deeply impressed one Sunday when the minister, preaching (as near as Aziz could recall) about the power of faith, had held an ice cube in his clenched fist as he addressed the congregation, demonstrating that faith in God could overcome pain and freezing cold. The minister had ended his sermon almost exactly at the moment when the ice cube was fully melted and he opened his hand showing the discoloration in his palm from the intense cold. When he went home Aziz had tried holding an ice cube for just one minute in his fist and he understood that the minister had the power of faith but that he did not. It hurt too much. His sophomore year in high school he stopped going to church.

He supposed that the fact that Tabitha was a Muslim was part of the reason he was here. They hadn't really asked him about that. During what seemed like hundreds of interrogations they had asked him over and over again about Tarique, about Tarique's friends, about the group of Muslims he played poker with on Thursday evenings.

Aziz's mother had been Muslim, his father a WASP from Peoria, Illinois. He had grown distant from them, even hostile as an adult, and it gave him a jolt of satisfaction to do a flip-flop on religion and marriage when he had announced his engagement to Tabitha. They couldn't complain about her religion or even about her being a foreigner, but they didn't like her very much.

Aziz was passionate about the out-of-doors. The best times he'd shared with his father — the only good times he remembered, really — were the times they'd gone trout fishing. When he was six or seven years old his father had taught him the rudiments of fly-casting and he'd spent the happiest hours of his childhood knee deep in icy cold streams, his father reminding him over and over again, "Keep that arm between ten o'clock and two o'clock. That's all it needs. Let the rod load up behind you before the forward cast." Aziz loved that feeling in the rod, and he loved to watch the tiny dimples in the water made by trout feeding on insects just beneath the surface, loved stalking them, creeping along the bank, keeping his profile low so the fish couldn't see him, loved the first cast when it landed right, three or four feet upstream of the rising trout, loved the splash when the fish came to his fly.

He was a wide-open-spaces man. On camping trips, when his buddies crawled into their tent, Aziz would stay in his sleeping bag outside, staring up at the moon or the stars or just the blackness, thinking about how much space there was, about how many cubic yards of air there must be in the world, how much acreage was all around them.

He particularly loved Montana. If Tabitha had not had so many members of her family in Milwaukee, they would have moved to Livingston or Bozeman, near some of the best trout streams in the west. The openness out there was breathtaking to Aziz. There was so much room and so few people. He couldn't imagine how people got — what was it? — agoraphobia, fear of open spaces. He was just the opposite.

Now he stared at the wall opposite, trying to see the gentle rapids of the Escanaba River spilling into a quiet pool where big trout waited.

"On your feet, Pendleton!" Aziz stood slowly and deliberately, steeling himself for the next interrogation. He would ask again to see a lawyer. They would tell him again that he was an enemy combatant and therefore had no right to see a lawyer. He would tell them that he was neither an enemy nor a combatant and therefore could not possibly be an "enemy combatant." They would ignore him and begin questioning him about the people he knew and spent time with. It would never end. They would go on shoving food through the slot in the cell door day after endless day, sending new people to ask him the same questions, locking him up again to stare at the four walls, with no windows, the light constant, no way to tell whether it was day or night outside except that he got a cup of lukewarm coffee in what he supposed was the morning, and something different later in the day (if it was day; he couldn't be sure).

Aziz hated the walls, hated the constant light spilling into his cell from the hallway, hated the closeness of his tiny cube that seemed to get smaller and smaller every day.

He held his hands through the gap in the bars for the cuffs. When the doors opened they shackled his feet. Two guards led him, shuffling, to the interrogation room. It wasn't always the same one. Today they took him to the one he preferred, where there were several chairs with soft seats, the only opportunity he had to sit on something that wasn't metal or the lumpy thin mattress of his bunk. He sat down. "I demand to see a lawyer."

"You're not entitled to a lawyer. You have been classified by Executive Order of the Department of Justice of the United States as an enemy combatant. As such, you will remain in our custody until we are convinced that you do not pose a threat to the government or people of the United States."

"I am neither an enemy nor a combatant. I have never been in combat in my life. I have never fired or used a weapon in my life. If I am not an enemy or a combatant, how can I be an enemy combatant?"

The part about firing a weapon was not quite true. When he was eleven, Aziz and his friend Willard had practiced firing Willard's new .22 rifle, and Aziz had shot at a neighbor's cat, hitting the butt end of its tail. The cat lived but most of its tail fell off, and Aziz had been deeply ashamed; he still was when he thought about it. As an adult he wouldn't touch a gun.

"Tell us more about the conversation you had with Tarique and Mohammed on the night of July 27."

"I've told you everything I can remember. We were playing poker. Tarique is not a very good poker player. He draws to inside straights. Mohammed is better, but reckless. We have been through this at least a hundred times."

Seventy-two days (or perhaps seventy-three). On many days there were two or three interrogations, so perhaps he had been through the poker game of July 27, 150 times or maybe 200 times.

Aziz had grown up with great respect for those in authority. He was taught that teachers and policemen and authors and judges must be respected, and he had always assumed that they were wise and decent as well. As a child he had often cried for hours when a teacher rebuked him, believing that he must be both wrong and bad. His mother had been little comfort, urging him to "be like a man."

In college he had been truly startled, even shocked, to discover over the course of his freshman year that two of his professors didn't know their subjects very well and taught them badly. His roommate, Lanny Cress, said, "So what's the big surprise? There are stupid professors. There are crooked cops. This is news to you?"

It *was* news to Aziz. He gradually learned, in his head, that these things were true, that people in positions of authority often did not deserve to be in those positions. But in his heart of hearts, he could never quite believe it. If the people in those positions weren't unusually smart and decent, why were they there?

Now the authorities had cast him out. The legal representatives of the highest authority in the land, the federal government, had classified him as an "enemy." He could never again be one of "We the people." They had made him into a "they." It wasn't even an accusation; rather he had been classified an enemy combatant by an authority that could not be questioned. He knew they were wrong, but if they were the Department of Justice, how could they be wrong? he wondered, and then he doubted himself. He longed, desperately, to talk to a friend, to a lawyer.

But they wouldn't let him speak to anyone. For the last ten weeks he had spoken only to people for whom he was a "they." Late in what he thought was the night, he wondered if they could somehow, in some crazy way, be right. Then, often, he wept.

Aziz looked up at his interrogator. "Tarique talked of Muslim rage." The words now tumbled out, by rote, repeated once again, the phrases identical to the times before. He had long since given up trying to create variations.

"I told him I wasn't a Muslim and I wasn't angry about anything much I could think of. I took the pot with a high pair, a pair of kings, I think. Tarique who, I freely admit, is not to be trusted, said that he *was* a Muslim and that he was angry. He showed me the gun he was carrying. I don't know what kind it was, except that it was a handgun, some kind of pistol. I asked him why he carried it. He said he might kill the infidels who were attacking Islam. I told him that was silly. I asked him, where were the infidels attacking Islam?

He said they're all over. I said that's silly, deal the next hand."

"Why didn't you report the gun to the police?"

"I had no reason to think it was illegal. One can get a permit to carry a handgun in Milwaukee. The administration is in favor of handguns."

"There was no permit for that gun. It was an illegal gun."

"How was I to know that? I'm not the police. You are the police."

The interrogation dragged on. Aziz answered more questions that he had answered many times before. Finally the interrogator said, "Well, that's it for today."

"I'm an American citizen," Aziz said. "I was born in the United States of America. I have some rights. I demand to see an attorney or to have a hearing before a judge or some court. I'm an American. I have that right."

"You are an enemy combatant — "

"Bullshit! I am no such thing! You know it. Don't you? Don't you?"

"We will see you tomorrow, Mr. Pendleton."

The interrogator stood up. Two guards lifted Aziz from the soft, covered seat of his chair. He shuffled between them back to his cell, wondering whether it was day or night, wondering whether it was day seventy-three or seventy-four. He would have to be more careful about marking the days on the wall next to his cot.

He would go fly fishing now. Soon he would see trout rising at the lower end of the south beaver pool on the Escanaba, right there. They were feeding on mayflies. A size fourteen Adams should do the trick.

On day 107 the wall started rotating again. The hourglass-shaped cockroach splatter was still the hub, the pivot. The wall was spinning clockwise, slowing down, reversing, and starting to turn counter-clockwise. Aziz watched, fascinated.

He had been thinking about his job. He wrote computer programs for Bissell Industries, a manufacturer of machine tools. Had they been informed where he was? Could he go back? After 107 days his job would be gone. And it wouldn't just be 107 days, it might be 170, or 225, or infinity, a concept he was coming to understand. They will take me back, he thought, they will take me back because I will explain that I have been detained as an enemy combatant and they will understand. They will be happy to have an enemy combatant at Bissell Industries. They love enemy combatants. I will show them what a good employee an enemy combatant can be! I will be good, I will be good. I will tell them everything I know and I will program computers. No. I will write programs for computers. No. I will compute programs, what's the right word?

On day 127 they opened the cell door. No handcuffs, no shackles. He looked at the guard, an inquiring expression, his head shaking slightly, his hands trembling. "You're being released today," the guard said.

"Released?"

"Yes."

"So I'm not an enemy combatant?"

"Come with me."

Aziz shuffled along the corridor. That was the way he had learned to walk outside his cell.

When they turned the corner he could see sunlight coming in through a window. He blinked. They led him to a room he hadn't seen before. They gave him back his clothes and his wallet and even his belt and his shoes. After he changed, he was led to the front of the prison. Tabitha was there, and his father. They appeared to be getting along cordially with one another, which surprised him. They jumped up and embraced him, both at the same time. "It was all a mistake," Tabitha said. "They admitted it. It was a mistake. It was Tarique and Mohammed they wanted, not you."

"You mean I'm not an enemy combatant?" He would ask them to say that, over and over again.

"Of course not!" His father laughed, a great hearty laugh that Aziz usually disliked, but it was reassuring now. "Enemy combatant. What nonsense."

"Please say that again," Aziz said.

"Say what?"

"Enemy combatant, what nonsense."

"It *is* nonsense —"

"Just say it!" His father looked at him queerly and repeated the phrase.

"Your father thinks we should sue the government," Tabitha said.

"No," Aziz said. "If I sue them I would be an enemy. I want to be We the People. It is very dangerous here. The wall spins. I will not be an enemy. I will not sue."

What's Happening Here

Following the dreadful events of 9/11/01, President Bush and his Attorney General, John Ashcroft, were quick to reassure the American people that the war against terrorism would not be fought at the cost of Americans' civil liberties. Administration policy statements took care to acknowledge that the terrorists would have won if America lost its open and democratic character.

We all recognize that there will be tension between some necessary security measures and civil liberties. But too often, when government began to creep after 9/11 and some of our most cherished constitutional rights began eroding, security was not enhanced. And Ashcroft's Department of Justice

(DOJ) saw little need to justify the sweeping new powers that it and the President assumed.

- Congress passed the USA Patriot Act in the month following the disaster. This act radically limits judicial oversight of FBI raids and surveillance of homes and offices, and permits new latitude for eavesdropping on e-mail and other electronic communications.

- An executive order from the President announced that terrorists would be tried by "military tribunals" with no appeal to the U.S. judicial system.

- New Justice Department guidelines gave FBI agents wider latitude to monitor libraries, Internet sites, and religious institutions without suspicion of criminal activity. "The FBI is now telling the American people, 'You no longer have to do anything unlawful to get that knock on the door,'" said Laura Murphy, director of the Washington Office of the ACLU.

- The DOJ announced that deportation hearings in "special interest" cases would be held in secret. Subsequently, more than 1,000 aliens were given secret hearings, and many of them were moved around the country so that their families and lawyers could not contact them.

- We learned that any persons designated "enemy combatants," a term that had no prior standing in law, could be detained indefinitely without access to a lawyer, without being charged with a crime, and without a hearing — even a hearing before a military court.

Thoughtful commentators from both wings of the political spectrum began speaking up.

"The danger of the so-called war on terrorism is that it will turn out to be what Mr. [vice president] Cheney and Mr. [secretary of defense] Rumsfeld say it is going to be, which is a permanent emergency," said Robert Higgs, a senior fellow in political economy at the Independent Institute in Oakland, California. "We may find that the administration continues to overstep onto people's constitutional rights, particularly their right to due process law, for a long time to come."

Stuart Taylor, Jr., a particularly thoughtful legal commentator, noted that the Bush Administration's self-declared rules — "the law according to Ashcroft" — meant that U.S. citizens like José Padilla and Yasser Esam Hamdi (one captured in Afghanistan, the other in Chicago) could be held in military brigs without being charged, without a lawyer, and without a hearing, for as long as the government wants.

"The Bush military-detention regime," Taylor says, "is part of a broader system of 'preventative detention' — incarceration of people who are neither convicted nor charged with any crime but who are perceived as dangerous — that the administration has been cobbling together. This system represents the sharpest departure since 9/11 from centuries of Anglo-American jurisprudence, and it is the most worrisome flirtation with police-statism."

As Robert A. Levy, senior fellow in constitutional studies at Washington's Cato Institute, wrote: "The Constitution does not distinguish between the protections extended to ordinary citizens on one hand and unlawful-combatant citizens on the other. The administration has decided that it will set the rules, prosecute infractions, determine guilt or innocence, then review the results of its own actions. That's too much unchecked power in the hands of the executive branch."

To their credit, the courts began putting on the brakes, though with considerable deference to the executive branch. In August of 2002 a three-judge panel of the U.S. Court of Appeals for the 6th Circuit in Cincinnati, noting that "Democracies die behind closed doors," ruled that the government must hold open deportation hearings for a Lebanese activist. He got such a hearing a few weeks later. But the 3rd Circuit, in early October, ruled the other way, upholding the government's right to secret hearings. At this writing the issue is unresolved.

The media and the public drew some lines too. When Ashcroft announced that the new Terrorism Information and Prevention System (TIPS) would ask mail carriers, meter readers, and UPS drivers to observe and report on suspicious activity in private homes, the outcry was immediate. The DOJ backed down and said it would confine this type of surveillance to public places.

Intrusions into our civil liberties must be justified by the government that's doing the intruding. When such policies really do make American citizens (and others) safer, some compromises may be appropriate. (Stuart Taylor recommends, for example, that detentions be limited to fixed periods of time, extendable only when justified by evidence.) But, in the war on terrorism, we must be particularly careful of government creep, because this war will have no end and governments have always used (and will always use) national emergencies — especially wars — to arrogate more and more power unto themselves.

CHAPTER THREE
Persecuted for "Pornography"

Billy Lee loved books. He had begun reading grown-up books as a young child and had tackled both the *Iliad* and the *Odyssey* his junior year in high school. When he graduated from college he naturally gravitated to a bookstore job — in Greenwich Village in New York.

As an employee, he was a bookstore owner's dream. He loved the merchandise he sold, knew which editions of a book were available and how to track them down. Customers sought his advice on their reading. If they liked Isaac Asimov, he would discuss which of Arthur C. Clarke's books might especially appeal to them. If they liked Melville, he could recommend some of Hawthorne's works. The result was prosperity for the store's owner, and three very satisfying years for Billy.

But he didn't really like the city. He hated the crowding, the traffic, the dirt, the noise. Where he grew up, in the hills of western Georgia, Billy was used to getting up in the morning and looking out at the soft colors of the Smoky Mountains, hearing the chattering of birds. He could be just as happy in winter, with the snow falling quietly, everything blanketed in silence, the bird songs now a sharp, tiny, intrusive sound in the whiteness.

So Billy headed back to Georgia, to the rolling hills where things were quiet, where people all knew each other, and life was likely to be uneventful but otherwise good, where the worlds of Homer, Ahab, Raskolnikov, and Huck Finn would blend easily and comfortably with the countryside and with Billy's reveries.

He settled in an isolated village tucked under the side of a forested mountain with a rock formation along the top that resembled the profile of a lion. A feeder from the Appalachian Trail led from the town up to this formation, called Lion's Head. From there one could see for many miles in three directions.

Billy took his savings from the Greenwich Village bookstore, borrowed some money from his uncle, and opened the Lion's Head Book Shop at the end of Maple Avenue, a narrow, tree-lined street about a quarter mile from the center of town. The center itself consisted of a drugstore with a soda fountain, a post office, a small grocery store, a liquor store, and a country inn that served *haute cuisine* dinners, mostly to tourists passing through, who found the inn's antique accoutrements so fascinating that they hardly noticed the pretentious, second-rate food.

Billy did not have a lot of customers, but some were regulars and, as he became increasingly expert in the classics, he began doing some out-of-town business through the mail. Soon people were taking advantage of his hard-to-find-book search service and his considerable knowledge about old books. He had to compete with the Internet but he also learned how to use research services on the Web to track down books and information for his customers.

He started making a little money. He knew it would never be a lot, but he was paying off the mortgage on the small building that housed his shop, and it looked as though he would be able to make enough to get by. In the spring he fished for native brook trout in the small but prolific

Wanachee River, which crossed the highway a mile south of town, and in the late fall hunting season he managed to kill a whitetail buck which provided a nice supply of venison for the winter. It seemed that this might be a pretty good life.

But maybe not for his girlfriend. Veronica had come with Billy from New York and they both had reservations about her life in rural Georgia. She was a city girl and she liked the noise and confusion and cacophony, as well as the many kinds of people the big city afforded and, especially, the privacy you could never have in a small town. But they agreed to give it a try. They were fond of each other, sexually enthusiastic together, and they trusted each other enough to put Veronica's experiment in country living on a trial basis. It seemed a risk worth taking.

At seven o'clock on a November evening, Billy closed up the Lion's Head Book Shop, locked the door, and began walking the three-quarter mile distance to the cottage — it was more like a cabin really — that he and Veronica shared. The first half-mile was reasonably well lit from the town's street lamps. The last part of the journey he enjoyed walking in the darkness, especially if there was a moon.

When he got to the cabin the telephone was ringing. Veronica was away visiting friends and had told Billy she would probably spend the night. Billy hurried into the house and grabbed the phone. "Hello?" There was a pause.

"Faggot!"

"What?" The phone clicked in his ear. Asshole, thought Billy. You don't expect to get crank calls in a small town. It seemed odd.

Billy put it from his mind. Five days later, as he and Veronica were having a supper of venison hash and a huge tossed salad laced with feta cheese, the phone rang again and Billy picked it up. Again the single word: "Faggot!"

"That's twice," Billy said. "Twice somebody has called up, said 'Faggot' and hung up. We've got a sicko in town somewhere."

"Maybe he's not in town," Veronica said. "Maybe it's one of our sicko friends from New York."

"I don't think so. Southern accent. Sounds like a redneck."

The next day, at 10:35 a.m. (he would remember the time exactly, because testimony about the time would be included in court records) a state trooper entered the Lion's Head Book Shop, asked Billy to identify himself, and informed Billy that he had a warrant to search for and confiscate all copies of a book entitled *Sand Dunes,* which contained child pornography.

"You've got to be kidding," Billy said. "There is no child pornography in this store. I wouldn't have it."

"Do you have *Sand Dunes*?"

"Yes. Three copies, I think."

"Give them to me." Billy rattled his ladder along its rail to the appropriate shelf, climbed up two steps, and pulled down his three copies of *Sand Dunes*.

He took the books to the trooper and said: "See? There's nothing pornographic here. Just kids on the beach, some nudity, that's all." He started to open the book and leaf through it. The trooper interrupted him.

"I'm not supposed to read them, I'm supposed to seize them. Give them to me. That's it."

"But I can show you."

"I don't need you to show me anything. These three books are being seized pursuant to a warrant executed by Judge Paul Dickerson on November 13. I'm confiscating the books. You may be indicted for child pornography."

"You're joking, surely."

The trooper turned and left, the three books gripped tightly under his arm. Billy closed up the Lion's Head Book Shop two hours early and went home.

"What was pornographic about it?" Veronica said.

"Nothing! I have never read that book all the way through. There are a few photographs of people in a nudist colony I think, but they're just playing on the beach. There are some poems; I think the book is mostly poetry. But it's ridiculous to suggest there's anything pornographic about it. It's high-toned stuff, expensive paper, poetry for God's sake!"

"In Lanier, Georgia, maybe it's high-toned, expensive-paper pornography," Veronica said.

"I can't believe that." The phone rang. "Yes?" said Billy.

"We don't lahk faggots around heah. Your trouble is jus' beginnin'." The caller hung up.

"It's the fucking Ku Klux Klan!"

"Jesus, Billy, maybe it is. You thought New York was dangerous, maybe it's more dangerous here."

A week later the Lion's Head Book Shop and Billy Lee were indicted on charges of child pornography relating to the possession with intent to sell one book entitled *Sand Dunes*, which "contains numerous examples of child pornography."

Lanier had three practicing lawyers, none of whom had much criminal experience, but one of them, Alan Cheshire, agreed to take Billy's case. He did some quick research on criminal procedures and on the child pornography statute. A hearing was scheduled before Judge Dickerson two weeks later. Alan sent for a copy of the book, so they could study it before the hearing. He was worried that even ordering the book and having it in his possession might subject him to some kind of criminal sanctions, but his colleagues felt that he would not be liable for prosecution if his sole purpose in obtaining the book was the defense of his client. They weren't sure, however. Maybe he could be thrown in jail. The law didn't say.

Once Alan made up his mind to take the case, he brought an unaccustomed degree of ferocity to it. His normal practice involved deeds, titles, and occasional corporate disagreements. Now he felt, having carefully gone through *Sand Dunes*, that a monumental injustice was being done, that free speech and the reputation of Georgia — indeed of the whole South — were at stake. "If they indict me, they indict me," he said to Billy. "I can't possibly defend you without studying the book, and I'm not going to pretend I don't have it."

Sand Dunes contained twelve photographs, most of them of adults on sand dunes, nude. The quality of the photographs was excellent, the shadows on the bodies and the dunes reflecting the photographer's obvious passion for texture and shape. Three of the photographs included children of various ages who were accompanied by adults who appeared to be their parents. There was no hint of sexuality or sexual play or lasciviousness about any of the photographs. They were basically studies of nude figures, alone and in groups.

Some of the poems were suggestive. The poetry had not, it appeared, been written to match the photographs but rather to sing the praises of nature, the out-of-doors, and, in a few cases, eroticism. This, Alan decided, was where the state would hang its case. There were photographs of children in the nude; there were poems that contained erotic suggestions, therefore this was child pornography. It was a stretch by anyone's definition, but Alan could see no other argument the state could make.

Sure enough, at the hearing before Judge Dickerson, the Assistant District Attorney folded out the pages containing the photographs of the nude families, then read aloud two of the poems, stressing the words "desire," "sensual," and "loins."

"Your Honor," the Assistant DA said, "The 'loins' referred to here are clearly the loins of that little girl — you can see right between her legs — on page thirteen, and probably the little boy there as well. This is just disgusting, your Honor. Poems designed to inflame lust in pedophiles and pictures that show the genitals of little children. Your Honor, this must be stamped out, this must be stopped, this must not be permitted in our great state. Our children must be protected!"

Alan Cheshire was not intimidated. He began: "Your Honor, there is nothing in this book that is obscene or pornographic. In order to find these photographs pornographic or obscene, you would have to find that the human body is itself obscene, and there is nothing in the law that demands that; there is nothing in the law that even permits that. The human body is not obscene. The human body is something we are all equipped with; God gave it to us, and it is good. To find those pictures pornographic would be to make us all obscene by definition. As to the poems, your Honor, those poems could never be found obscene or pornographic anywhere. They don't even contain four-letter words. There is nothing dirty about them. They do not describe sexual acts. They do not advocate sexual acts or sexual activity of any kind.

"In addition, your Honor, it would place an unreasonable burden, an extraordinarily unreasonable burden on the owner or on the manager of any bookstore anywhere in this state if he or she had to read every single word of every single book in order to ascertain even the remote possibility that a poem, a perfectly innocent-sounding poem, might somehow be interpreted by somebody somewhere as pornographic.

"Your Honor, I submit that there will be no more bookstores in this state, that intellectual life, artistic and cultural life in our state will be crushed if you find this book to be child pornography. Every bookseller will have to clean out all their books, every single one of them, including the dictionary and the Bible, because those volumes, your Honor, contain words and scenes and images that Mr. Singer here claims to find pornographic. I urge you to dismiss this case at once."

The judge found *Sand Dunes* to contain child pornography. Alan advised Billy that he was entitled to a jury trial, and that a jury would, in all likelihood, find him not guilty, but there were no guarantees. There would probably be rednecks on the jury, "the bubba crowd" as Alan called them, and they would probably not be reasonable on this subject. Furthermore, a jury trial would cost a good many thousands of dollars that Billy did not have. Billy and Alan decided to let Alan see if he could work out a plea agreement with the District Attorney's office. The DA insisted that the Lion's Head Book Shop be closed as a condition of any plea.

When Billy got home that night he found a letter addressed to him in a scrawling, childlike hand. The letter said: "We got you fagot. You like them peenies in that book? We'll close your fagot store."

Billy took the letter to Ralph Delaney, Lanier's sheriff, whose office was next door to the District Attorney's. Billy told Delaney about the phone calls, and gave him the letter. "I wish I had time to investigate every crank call I get complaints about, every crank letter," Ralph Delaney said. "But there are just too many cranks in the world to go after all these things. If anything serious occurs, you come to me, Billy, and I'll look into it. But I can't spend my time on these threats. This doesn't even threaten anything violent. Sorry."

Billy pointed out that there was almost certainly a connection between the threats and his indictment. Sheriff Delaney said he had another, more urgent matter to attend to.

Billy decided to accept the plea, close the Lion's Head Book Shop, and leave town. It made him boil inside, because he knew that his departure and the closure of his shop meant that the "faggot" man had won, that the sicko with "peenies" on his brain was the victor, that bigotry and prudery and stupidity had triumphed over civilization and literature and tolerance, but he didn't have the money to pay for a trial and he didn't really have the stomach for it either.

Veronica went back to New York.

What's Happening Here

A major problem with child pornography laws, and with the broader obscenity laws as well, is that they are vague. Because they are vague, they tend to be applied by prosecutors or others with agendas of their own — agendas that frequently have nothing to do with the application of justice or with protecting children. Child pornography laws have been used, for example, to prosecute books and videos containing sexual activity by mature seventeen-year-olds who forged identification to prove their adulthood. This is clearly a very different matter from the sort of protection society wishes to maintain for prepubescent children. Similarly, child pornography laws, because they prohibit "lewd" or "lascivious" depictions involving children, are open to a wide variety of interpretations. Hence, in numerous cases, simple nudity has been found illegally pornographic.

For example, the Barnes & Noble bookstore chain was under indictment in Montgomery, Alabama, in 2002, for selling a book of nude photographs very similar to the one described in Billy's story. The book, *Radiant Identities*, is by photographer Jock Sturges, whose photographs hang in the Metropolitan Museum of Art, among other places. It does not include even a hint of sexual activity or lasciviousness, and most of us would consider it entirely innocent and acceptable. Yet one of America's largest book chains may be heavily fined and some of its employees thrown in jail for selling it.

Similarly, in 1988, Alice Sims, an artist in Alexandria, Virginia, was subjected to a nightmare of prosecutorial abuse for having taken photographs of her own children in the altogether. Police searched her home, confiscated artwork and personal records, and then had the child welfare authorities seize Sims's two small children, placing them in protective custody. A film processor had reported to the police that photographs that Sims had taken of her daughter and a friend in the bathtub, for a series of paintings called "Water Babies," might be child pornography. It took Sims and her husband and a lawyer a good many weeks and a good deal of money to settle the matter.

In Tulsa, Oklahoma, in 1997, copies of the Oscar-winning German film *The Tin Drum* were seized by zealous prosecutors following an advisory opinion by Oklahoma County District judge Richard Freeman. The film had received international acclaim over nearly three decades before anyone in Oklahoma, or elsewhere, found anything pornographic in a brief scene that was, at most, suggestive of sexual activity. In this case too, defenders of the First Amendment eventually won the argument, but only at great cost to the many parties involved and to the greater interests of art and artistic filmmaking.

The thoughtful British magazine *The Economist* points out that Americans are not quite normal when it comes to children and their bodies. "In fact, they are off the charts, at least compared with most Europeans. The simplest place to observe this is on the beach. In Europe, toddlers commonly run around naked, and nobody cares or pays attention. In America, people are easily shocked, and soon tell parents to cover the kids up." This same article noted a case in which New Jersey police took three children from their home on a winter's night in 1994 after a lab had handed in photographs taken by their father showing his six-year-old daughter nude. "The father explained that the pictures were for his amateur photography class, but he and his family went through a year of hell before the case against him was dropped."

In one case it was held that even depictions of children who were clothed could constitute child pornography. An "expansive" interpretation of the federal statute resulted in the conviction of Stephen Knox for having videotapes of young girls in bathing suits, leotards, and the like. The Third U.S. Circuit Court of Appeals upheld Knox's conviction, asserting that an illegal exhibition of the pubic area could be found even when clothing completely covered it if the photographer "unnaturally" focused on it.

Demonstrating just how far America's lawmakers can go in their zeal to "protect children," Senator Ken Arnold of the Colorado legislature tried to pass a law that defined child pornography to include anything a judge might deem to be lascivious. As an example of the "lascivious" art he wanted to ban, Arnold pointed to a picture of a young girl standing fully dressed next to a pick-up truck containing a dead deer, and stated, "Look at that. It's like abuse is okay." The *Denver Post* editorialized that they weren't quite sure what Senator Arnold's problem was with deer hunting but noted that just this kind of thing is likely to result from broad interpretations of vague laws.

Similar vagueness and similar abuses attend the adult obscenity laws. Sexual depictions, under current Supreme Court decisions, are protected under the First Amendment unless they meet all three of the following criteria: the material taken as a whole must be "patently offensive" to contemporary community standards (community is not defined); the material must appeal to a "prurient interest" in sex, meaning an unnatural or unhealthy interest in sex rather than a normal interest; the material must be lacking in artistic, scientific, literary, or political value. These vague criteria have resulted in a legal climate within which, as one observer has put it, the only way to be sure one is operating within the law is "to read the thoughts of a jury not yet impaneled in a case not yet called in connection with a citation not yet issued for a transaction not yet made." It has also re-sulted in thousands of prosecutions, the expenditure of vast sums of taxpayer monies, and the suppression of a great deal of sexually oriented material that most Americans would consider perfectly acceptable for adult reading or viewing.

Obscenity laws thus create a situation in which one set of people is deciding on the sexual content of entertainment and art for everybody else. In a free society no group of people, including legislators and judges, has the right to dictate the content of reading, art, and entertainment for others.

CHAPTER FOUR
The Welfare Trap

"I'm not going to let welfare become a way of life," Teresa said to Bert. "In the first place, the rules have changed. To get the payments, you have to be looking for work or taking training, and besides, there's a five-year limit. So it just can't be a way of life anymore. But that's not the main point. The main point is I don't *want* welfare. Taking a handout makes me feel sick inside, deep down. I just don't like it."

"I don't get it," Bert said. "It's no handout. It's your right. All the government workers say that. You got a right to a minimum income. So do I. It's the government's money. The government has millions. Why shouldn't we be able to lead a decent life? We need the money."

"The government's not some space alien, Bert. The government gets its money from people," Teresa shot back. "We had to attend a workshop about this last Thursday. One of the welfare workers got pretty worked up about it. She told us: 'I pay taxes. The government takes my money. When the government takes my money and gives some of it to you, I am supporting you. I don't mind doing that in the case of serious need, but I work hard, sometimes I work real hard for my salary, and nearly twenty percent of it goes to the government for government programs, and I don't think the government should take my money to give it to people who aren't out there hustling their butts to get a job.' "

"She's talking bullshit," said Bert. "That just serves her own thing. She's tryin' to show she's better than you are. She's no better, believe me. A lot of those social workers goof off. I know, I've goofed off with them sometimes. Besides, the baby's getting older. We've got to keep shoes on the kid."

"Yes, we've got to keep shoes on the kid. That means we've got to earn the money to buy the shoes."

"Jobs aren't so easy to get," Bert said.

"You seem to get the summer jobs pretty easy."

"I can get the summer jobs," Bert said. "That's outdoor work. I like it. Usually lasts for five or six months and then I can get unemployment for three or four months more."

"Don't you think it's wrong to work the system that way?"

"What's working the system? You want to make a living, you want to get by, you follow the rules, you get by. There's nothing good about it or bad about it, you just get by. That's the way the system works."

Teresa and her eighteen-month-old baby, Mario, lived in a modest railroad apartment over Henderson's store in Reden City, West Virginia. In the old days Henderson's had been known as "Henderson's Dry Goods Store," but they now sold a little bit of everything, from cigarettes and groceries to fishing licenses to latté and cappuccino prepared right behind the counter.

The owner, Buddy Arsenault, a great nephew of the original Mr. Henderson, was pleased to have Teresa as a tenant. She'd been there for a year since having her baby and moving out of her parents' place over on Trumbull Street. Teresa always paid her rent on time, she was quiet, and Buddy was sure she took good care of the place. She got welfare for the baby — AFDC Buddy thought it was — and that seemed to provide a pretty reliable source of income.

Buddy wasn't so sure about her boyfriend. He knew Bert. He and Bert's father used to go bass fishing together when Bert's father worked unloading food trucks for the IGA and before they moved up to Wheeling, where there were better jobs. Bert had a reputation as a pretty good bass fisherman himself, but he also seemed to Buddy to be a goof-off. He got forest service jobs in the summertime but for half the year he didn't seem to do anything much at all, except hang around Teresa, drink beer, and, Buddy figured, probably get into illegal drugs to boot. Buddy had a hard time with young men who were just hanging around. He didn't see how any young, able-bodied man, or woman for that matter, could just hang around. There was something unhealthy about it. •

Teresa, now, that was a different matter. She was always moving around and busy; she seemed to have somewhere to go and something to do, even with that baby.

"Don't you feel better when you're working?" Teresa asked Bert. "Doesn't the day go by faster, don't you feel like you're more somebody when you're working, earning your paycheck?"

"Not especially. I mean, I don't mind living half the time with my uncle and half the time here. That works out okay. If I can get the unemployment, and you can get your check so we can feed the baby, and I can get the forest service work again in the summer, no, I don't see the difference between working and not working as long as there's enough money to get by."

"Well it bothers me to see you lurking around all the time, especially during working hours during the week. It just bothers me, that's all," Teresa said.

"I'll go fishing then. Maybe if I'm fishing that will look better to you than hanging around." Bert picked up his spinning rod and a couple of purple plastic worms and headed down the back steps to his pickup. He didn't understand all this stuff about work. You did what you had to do. He liked Teresa and he was crazy about the baby. It was a pretty good life. Let other people worry about the "work ethic." Corporations got subsidies, farmers got subsidies, why shouldn't he get a break? At Henderson's he picked up a six-pack of beer and a coffee cup full of nightcrawlers to go with his plastic worms. He spent the rest of the afternoon fishing and drinking beer.

The following April, Bert was late for his appointment to sign up for the forest service job. The chief ranger, who liked Bert, figured he could still get him into one of the summer slots, but there were a lot of applicants that year and the hiring process was more formal and better recorded than usual. Reluctantly, the ranger told Bert he hadn't made the cut.

"What do you mean? I've been doing this job every year for four years."

"I know that," said the ranger. "But this time you had to be here on time. You knew that. You had to get your application on the stack with the others before noon. Yours was late. I tried to move it up, but I couldn't without getting into trouble. I'm sorry."

Later at Teresa's apartment, Bert said, "It's 'screw Bert' year. Everybody's unloading on me. Without the summer work, I won't be able to collect unemployment."

"You can work at the IGA. Unloading trucks."

"That job sucks. Minimum wage. Five bucks an hour. I don't have to do that." He paused. "How much have we got coming in?"

"With my afternoon shift at K-Mart, the baby and I can get by. We can pay the rent as long as the welfare worker looks the other way about my job. Thank God I can leave Mario with mother while I'm working. But you've got to do something. The AFDC and food stamps are getting cut back but the expenses are growing. So you've got to work."

"Shit."

Bert worked for two weeks unloading food trucks at the IGA, then he quit. "I don't have to do that kind of work," he told Teresa.

He started drinking boilermakers. Soon he began to look forward to his first drink — around two or three in the afternoon — as the high point of the day. Getting drunk, at least a little bit drunk, became the principal focus of his life.

What's Happening Here

For Bert, there is little chance of becoming a complete — or happy — human being. When one depends on another who is in turn dependent on a government check, a sense of identity or self-worth is nearly impossible.

We rarely recognize the extent to which human happiness requires struggle. From the time we learn language as children, through the times we learn how to ride a bike and make a living in a complex world, our sense of self-worth comes from overcoming genuinely difficult obstacles. Language, bike riding, earning a living — these are all difficult and challenging tasks. As we address, one by one, the many obstacles to accomplishing them, we begin to value ourselves, to give ourselves credit for being competent and worthwhile human beings. As we pursue difficult objectives, we feel fully alive. A poet laureate, Robert Pinsky, summed this up, noting "We crave difficulty." Chess players are bored with checkers. A professional tennis player gets no pleasure from beating a beginner.

When essential challenges like earning a livelihood are not part of what we do, life loses its sense of structure and much of its joy. "People have a deep need for the sense of competence that comes from mastering something that is difficult," notes sociologist and author Charles Murray. For Bert, this whole aspect of human happiness is absent.

Bert is right, of course, that there are even less worthy recipients of government beneficence. When we engage in the insupportable practice of subsidizing corporate giants like Archer Daniels Midland or millionaire sugar growers in Florida, it can seem hypocritical to oppose welfare such as Aid to Families with Dependent Children. The answer is to eliminate both forms of welfare because both are destructive. Subsidized corporations bleed the taxpayers for the benefit of a few wealthy officers and shareholders. Welfare for individuals enervates and renders miserable the "beneficiaries" of its own largesse.

At the turn of the current century thousands of welfare recipients were interviewed by the press after getting out of the welfare system and finding work. Virtually none expressed a wish to return to the old life. In many cases this was true even if they had less money from their jobs than they had gotten on welfare, and even if day care for their children was a heavy burden. Happiness, for most people, requires the effort of productive activity.

CHAPTER FIVE
The Price of Federal Handouts

"We'll never be able to make it without the federal funds," Theresa Dolittle said to the other members of the board. "We get $1.5 million from these three grants. They've been pretty reliable and they cover a lot of our base salaries, as well as critical program costs. I just don't see how we'll be able to carry on without them."

"I think we can do it," said Ralph Delancy. Ralph was a senior board member and president of the local bank. He had achieved his position through hustling and hard work, and he was inclined to think that these qualities could also save Landsdowne Charities and their Community Development Program.

Landsdowne Charities had humble beginnings. Initiated by Arnold L. Landsdowne during the Depression, it had focused on helping indigent members of the community, particularly widows with young children.

Over the years, as the Depression became a memory and the threat of starvation began to recede, Landsdowne Charities took up a variety of community development programs. These included adult literacy projects, a treatment component that dealt with alcohol dependency, and teen counseling centers for young adults with substance abuse problems.

The expanding menu of services attracted federal support; indeed, some of the services offered were designed specifically to take advantage of the availability of federal funding. As the federal resources became more reliable, the development committee of Landsdowne's board of directors relaxed a bit about the necessity of raising private funds, and support from private sources consequently diminished.

The federal funds had certain costs for the organization. Department of Health and Human Services requirements involved not only a vigorous independent auditing of Landsdowne's accounts, but very substantial reporting, which included filling out numerous forms, providing detailed justifications for any changes in key personnel, strictly conforming to a variety of federal regulations and laws (some of which seemed to contradict others), and persistently subjecting the charity's records and staff to federal audits and inspections. Landsdowne Charities had developed systems and hired staff to cope with these requirements, however, and as a result, had become somewhat bureaucratized, somewhat less "private," and considerably less inclined to do anything risky, anything that might conceivably run afoul of the mass of federal regulations.

In 1992 Landsdowne decided it would remodel one of its buildings to create a new teen counseling center. Most of the cost could be borne by the ongoing federal grants; the grant conditions for "construction" would apply.

The charity had an across-the-board nondiscrimination policy, guaranteeing in statements displayed at two conspicuous places on its premises that it would not discriminate on the basis of race, gender, or sexual preference. But when it came time to hire the contractors for the remodeling, the grant conditions mandated that minority- or women-owned businesses should be given preference for the work.

This issue produced a hot debate at the next board meeting.

Ralph Delancy and two of his business-oriented colleagues were lined up against Theresa Dolittle and Mary Runkle, Landsdowne's Executive Director.

"This kind of preference is fair," Mary insisted. "It gives struggling new businesses a chance."

"I have no problem with giving preference to struggling new businesses," Ralph said. "But that's not the policy they're insisting on. This system says we have to give preference to women and minority-owned businesses even if they're the biggest and oldest contracting businesses in town."

"They aren't," Mary said, and Theresa nodded.

"Sometimes principles matter," Ralph said. "Our nondiscrimination policy is fundamental. When we discriminate in favor of anyone, we automatically discriminate against someone else. This will be a divisive action in this community. Any nonminority contractor who might have otherwise won the contract, and who fails to get this work because of our discrimination, will feel cheated, and rightly so. I can't go along with it."

But Theresa and Mary stood their ground, supported by Landsdowne's lawyer, Peter Sharp. "Now that HHS has specifically brought this to our attention," Sharp told them, "we can't ignore it. We're going to have to discriminate in favor of minority- and women-owned businesses, for this particular job at the very least. Otherwise we'll be subject to fines or other reprisals."

"Then I don't think we should do this work," Ralph said. "We don't have to. We can provide the same services from a rental facility. Let's do that."

After the board decided to postpone the decision, Ralph shared his growing conviction that Landsdowne was becoming overly bureaucratized with one of his allies on the Board, Vicky Warwick. "The discrimination thing has reminded me," he said to Vicky, "that Landsdowne seems to be getting awfully 'federalized.'"

"I know it," Vicky said. "We're hiring a lot of people just to satisfy the government's requirements. They all have nice-sounding titles, like 'program officer,' and 'accounting assistant,' but most of what they do seems to be unnecessary."

"I think we're losing Landsdowne's independent, risk-taking nature and turning into a little government," Ralph said at the next board meeting. "Our staff seem to just be playing it safe. Their priority is making sure that we remain eligible for federal funds when it should be doing things that are useful for the people of this community." Vicky nodded vigorously and quickly spoke up.

"We've got to do things the way we believe they should be done," she said, "the way that will benefit the people of this community, whether that conforms with all this federal nonsense or not."

Vicky and Ralph made it clear that they were prepared to resign from the board over this matter and, in combination, their voices were powerful. They were the only two board members who were rich enough to make significant contributions to the "unrestricted fund" of the organization, and this was Landsdowne's most flexible operating money.

The others, especially Mary Runkle, recognized that without Vicky and Ralph the organization would become even more bureaucratized, less independent, and more and more like a "branch of the Department of Health and Human Services," as Vicky put it. Mary was worried.

The battle raged through one more board meeting before the full board met in mid-October and the tide turned in

Vicky and Ralph's favor. Vicky had taken Mary Runkle out to lunch three times during the previous two months, and she argued her case persuasively. The two women had also visited a small new nonprofit that Vicky had helped start, and Mary had been reminded of how dynamic, exciting, and responsive a small private organization could be. By the time of the October board meeting, Mary had been won over.

The board decided that Landsdowne would not do the remodeling with federal funds, or perhaps at all; more dramatically, Ralph and Vicky, now backed by Mary, proposed a program to wean the organization from all federal support, restoring it to the status of a real private charity.

"How can we survive without the federal funds?" Theresa asked. "One-and-a-half million is a lot of money. We can't replace that."

"We can try," Vicky said. "Ralph and I will dig a little deeper into our own pockets." She looked directly at Ralph. "Won't we?"

"Yes," he said. "And more importantly, we'll get out there and organize some serious fundraising. For the last few years we've been resting on our oars."

Mary Runkle spoke up. "Staff morale is weakening," she said. "That's the main reason I've changed my mind on this. We're turning into a federal proposal factory and losing sight of our bottom-line goals."

"I understand that this is a big step," Ralph said. "Maybe no other organization has given up federal support voluntarily. You're putting a lot of faith in Vicky and me to make up for at least some of that money. By the way," he said to Mary, "how much of the $1.5 million in federal funding do you really think we'll have to make up with private money?"

"I've been doing some calculating," Mary said. "It would be really nice to make it all up, of course, but we may not have to. First of all, I figure we've got three people on the payroll we won't need if we don't have the federal reporting requirements. Actually, they're underworked, and with their benefits added in, this will save us about $160,000 right off the bat. Then there are three other clerical staff I should have let go some time ago. But it's so hard to fire people, and there was just never a real justification before. Once I notify staff that we will be receiving no new federal funds and that we'll have to downsize, I think those three can be terminated. To be perfectly blunt about it, the organization is likely to be better off without them — they've been goofing off and the others resent it. That saves us another $100,000.

"In addition, all of our federally-funded, program-related services automatically cost more — I figure at least twenty-five percent more because of the federal requirements, the cash flow problems, and resulting interest payments. I asked both of our senior field program supervisors how much in completely private and discretionary funds they would need to operate the service programs that now cost about $500,000 per year. They both said they could probably accomplish the same level of service with $350 or $400 thousand in discretionary funds. I was skeptical about this, but they explained it in some detail and I believe them.

"Then there are a lot of intangibles. People will work harder when we're lean and mean. I figure if we can raise $900,000 in private funds, we can keep a level of services comparable to what we provided with the $1.5 million in federal funding."

"I think we can handle that," Ralph said. "I think we can manage that."

The next day Mary posted a large notice on Landsdowne's bulletin board. It read:

DECLARATION OF INDEPENDENCE

At yesterday's Board of Directors meeting, it was decided that Landsdowne Charities, starting in July of next year, will accept no more federal funds for any of our programs. While this will clearly impose hardships over the short term, including downsizing of the organization, the Board believes, and I agree, that we will be able to conduct many of our community development and charitable activities as well or better if we are able to raise even half the missing funds from the private sector. We will be more flexible, we will be more innovative, we will be less bureaucratic. We will once again feel encouraged to take risks on behalf of those who need our services, including such things as abortion counseling, a hotline for battered women, and charging fees for some of our meals.

We will have to work harder. We will have to work smarter. Landsdowne will have to become lean and mean, with no wastage. No more leaving the lights on unnecessarily, no more paying a little extra for products and services "because it isn't our money anyway." From now on it will be our money and we'll pinch every nickel.

I know I can count on you and I'm looking forward to working with you in the new liberated Landsdowne Charities.

Landsdowne's transformation went better than expected. Vicky and Ralph put together a committee of sixteen local businesspeople, community leaders, and foundation executives. In the first eighteen months after the conversion took place, they raised two million dollars.

Without the dead weight of the federal hand, staff meetings began to buzz with new ideas, zany, creative ideas, many of which were too far off the charts to implement, but a few of which represented real innovation in the community development world. Inspired by the new atmosphere, staff members who had previously punched the clock began showing up early and staying late. Landsdowne Charities, pretty much to the surprise of all concerned, became a lively and interesting place to work.

What's Happening Here

Just as welfare has so often created a psychology of dependence among the individuals who receive cash payments, so government funds can undermine the strength and dynamism of private organizations. Government — that is, taxpayers' — funding must necessarily come with a great many strings attached; when an organization's funding is being provided by all of the American people, collectively, the organization is answerable in many different ways, some of which may be incompatible with a charitable organization's objectives or with promoting a productive workplace in which ideas can flourish.

Federal funding for the arts provides a good example. This subject arouses passionate controversy, partly because some people don't like having their taxes used to support art or other work that offends them. Virginia Postrel, author of *The Future and Its Enemies*, has pointed out that the first televised episodes of *Tales of the City*, a series with strong sexual content, were highly controversial because they were shown on public television; later episodes, which contained even more nudity and franker discussions of homosexuality, aroused little controversy because they appeared on a private network, with no taxpayer funds involved.

As we have seen at Landsdowne Charities, government funding also frequently promotes waste. In my nonprofit work I have often observed the "it-isn't-our-money-anyway" psychology, which results in paying more than necessary for goods and services, hurriedly "spending the budget," and swelling overheads. The idea that the government's money can be wasted (as long as it is wasted in strict accordance with the regulations, which virtually never require thrift) is pernicious; not only is this money down the drain, but everyone involved becomes a little less disciplined, a little less moral.

In addition, the psychology of dependence can begin to permeate a private organization to the point that it loses sight of what it is in business to do and instead devotes much of its energy to maintaining the flow of federal funds, even when this means changing program focus, adding less-than-dedicated staff, or embracing new politically popular areas of "social need" which may not be important in a given community.

For universities, there is yet another danger: the government calls the tune on research, deciding what needs to be researched and what doesn't. The process inevitably reflects government biases. If, for example, the government's position on drug control is that marijuana is a dreadfully harmful substance, then it will fund research that is likely to reinforce this position. Very little research will be funded, at least by the government, if it is likely to support the opposite conclusion (which is, in fact, the correct one: the active ingredients in marijuana turn out to be among the safest and least harmful substances so far discovered. The respected medical journal *The Lancet*, for example, reviewed thirty years of research in 1995 and concluded that "the smoking of cannabis, even long term, is not harmful to health.").

Organizations that operate with private funds are thus less wasteful, more efficient, and more flexible than government-sponsored institutions. This is not because government is inherently evil, it is because of the way governments function.

CHAPTER SIX
Police Power

When the police broke through the bedroom door, Myrna and Gino were making love. Under the force of two hurtling bodies, the door exploded inward with a loud, shocking bang. The explosion was followed by a crashing sound as the door, hanging by one hinge, smashed back against the wall. Myrna and Gino jumped apart, both trying to cover themselves with the top sheet. Four policemen swarmed into the room, two in black SWAT team jackets, pistols held at the ready, yelling "Freeze!" Gino raised his hands above his head. Myrna, holding the sheet in front of her, raised her hands as high as she could.

"You, over there on the floor! Face down!" the lead cop ordered Gino, shoving him toward the narrow space between the bed and the far wall. Gino, naked, rolled off the bed onto the floor face down, his hands extended above his head. "Hands behind your waist!"

Gino put his hands behind his back. The cop jerked them together, jammed Gino's right wrist into a metal handcuff, then cuffed the other hand. He was kneeling in the middle of Gino's back.

Myrna was forced to lie down on the floor at the foot of the bed, where she too was handcuffed, face down, her nakedness only partly covered by the sheet one of the policemen threw over her buttocks.

The entire episode had taken less than two minutes. The first cop still had a knee in the middle of Gino's back. He now grabbed him by the hair, twisted his head and leaned down and yelled into his face, "Where's the coke? Where is it?"

"I don't know what you're talking about!" said Gino. "There's nothing here. I swear it. I don't use drugs. You've made a mistake!" He was almost screaming.

"Search the place, and I mean search it!" said the cop who appeared to be in charge. "Boyd, tell Barbara to come up and body search the woman."

Over the next few minutes, the apartment was systematically destroyed. Myrna wept as she heard them tearing into the embroidered pillowcases and settee cover just outside the bedroom. She had worked long and hard at her sewing machine with some especially fine Kashmiri crewelwork that she had brought half-way around the world from a vacation ten years before.

The police sliced the couch open, emptied and overturned the drawers, swept clothing and papers onto the floor. Then they turned to a painting Gino treasured, a portrait of Myrna that he had bought from an artist friend, which had a sealed paper back, creating a space between the canvas and the paper. Gino heard one of the cops slash at the paper with a knife, then the sickening sound of canvas tearing. "Whoops! Got her right in the kisser," the cop said.

Gino felt a wave of nausea as he heard the destruction go on. "Check the globe light, Rutter," he heard.

"I can't get the son of a bitch unfastened."

"Break it."

Policewoman Barbara Smoltz led Myrna to the bathroom, where she examined her naked body for any possible sign of drugs, probed her anus and vagina with a gloved finger, helped her into her bathrobe, and ordered her to sit at the kitchen table where she was told not to move. Myrna was shaking uncontrollably. She had seen that they had sliced open the toothpaste tubes in the bathroom, and emptied out all the medicine bottles and cosmetic containers. In the kitchen they had emptied three bottles of wine, a tin of coffee, and the entire contents of her cupboard and refrigerator, all dumped into the sink and on the floor. She could barely bring herself to speak. "You pigs," she whispered. "There's nothing here, don't you understand there's nothing here? You have absolutely no right."

"We have a search warrant," Officer Smoltz said. "We have a report that this is a drug scene. That's all we need."

"And if you're wrong?"

"We're not wrong."

The radio on the belt of the officer-in-charge crackled. "Briant, Holt, are you there? Over. Briant."

The cop in charge spoke quickly into it: "Briant here."

"Our informant has changed his story. Now he's saying it's 110 Wilson Avenue, not Wilton Avenue. Wilson makes more sense anyway. We better regroup."

"Okay," said Officer Briant into the radio. "Not a problem. We got these two on sodomy at least. Over."

Myrna jumped up. "I told you you were making a mistake!"

"We have a search warrant, lady. We're here legally. And when we got here you were committing a crime."

Officer Barbara Smoltz broke in: "Oh come on."

"What do you mean?" Briant demanded. "She was sucking his dick when we secured the bedroom. That's sodomy. A felony. We'll get them on it, and it gives us leverage."

"Are you crazy?" Myrna yelled. "You come in here and destroy my home, invade my body, because you're too stupid to find the right fucking address! And now you're going to throw up some idiot law that says how we can have sex? You've got to be kidding!"

"You'll see if I'm kidding, lady," said Briant. "Judge Boyce is pretty hard on sodomy cases. He's big on family values, and he doesn't like perversion of any kind. We'll make it stick. We've got two witnesses."

A few days later, Myrna and Gino prepared to sue the city. They took pictures of the black-and-blue marks on Gino's shoulder where he had been shoved into the wall, his bruised wrists, and the cuts on his face. They photographed the shambles that was the apartment. A week after they filed the suit, the prosecutor went before a grand jury to seek a sodomy indictment against them.

"I can't believe this. I really can't believe this." Myrna said. She and Gino were having a discussion with their attorney.

"It's an unusual combination, I'll admit," the attorney said. She was a courtly, soft-spoken, middle-aged woman named Regina Middleton, and while her demeanor and her experience were reassuring, her words were not. "It's true that prosecutors don't normally bring sodomy charges against heterosexual couples in connection with drug busts," she said. "Sodomy charges themselves are relatively rare, and they tend to be brought most frequently against homosexuals. But in this state anal and oral sexual contact is a crime, even for married couples.

"I don't get it," Gino said. "During Clinton's impeachment, even the conservative politicians were saying that sex is a sin, not a crime. They said the President's lying was a crime, but not the sex."

"That's what they said, but it's not true," Middleton said. "Consensual sodomy is still a crime in Virginia, right across the river from Washington, for example. And you've read about all the military prosecutions for adultery. We have a double standard, and that means a double whammy right now. I'm a little surprised this DA is going for sodomy, though. When they blow a drug case the police usually charge their targets with resisting arrest. Calling them pigs could have been enough. They'll probably throw that in if we press the lawsuit."

"We didn't resist arrest," Myrna protested.

"It's an easy claim for the police to make. They got a seventy-four-year-old woman for resisting arrest at a peaceful protest in New York when she hadn't resisted at all," Middleton replied. She sorted through her stack of papers. "And a man named William Fry was jailed in North Carolina for more than two years for having consensual oral sex with his girlfriend. Even fornication and adultery are getting enforced from time to time when the police can use them tactically."

Myrna and Gino exchanged disbelieving glances.

"If we go to trial I don't believe a jury would *want* to convict you of sodomy. It's simply too outrageous. On the other hand, we'd be in a bind. If I put you on the stand — which I'd like to because I think you'd both be sympathetic witnesses — you'd have to admit having oral sex. The judge, particularly if it's Boyce, might very well instruct the jury in such a way as to virtually require that they find you guilty. If I don't put you on the stand, it's just the word of the two police witnesses against whatever I can do to undermine their testimony. But if they saw fellatio, or even something close, we'd have a problem. The law prohibits absolutely any contact between the mouth of one person and the genitals of another person. It also prohibits penis-anal and oral-anal contact. It's a crazy law. Idiotic, really, when you consider that sex therapists are urging elderly clients to experiment with different kinds of sexual activity, particularly oral sex. But there it is. We can't change the law."

"Could we really be sent to jail for this?" Myrna asked.

"I'm afraid so."

"It seems especially crazy for cunnilingus," Gino said. "I've always thought I was being politically correct."

"Whatever," Myrna said.

"This is a serious matter," Regina said. "And yes, cunnilingus is included. The moment your tongue or lips touch the vulva — the labia, clitoris, or any part of the genitalia — you have committed a felony, a crime more serious in this state than many forms of theft or assault."

"It's unbelievable," Myrna said.

"At least we no longer burn witches. I'm going to meet with the District Attorney tomorrow and I'll see what he's willing to offer. If they'll drop the sodomy charges in exchange for your giving up the lawsuit, I will probably recommend that you agree. It's unfair and it's unjust, but given the risks here, it may be the best we can do."

Regina was right about the negotiation. The District Attorney offered to drop the sodomy charges if Myrna and Gino would cancel their lawsuit. Regina urged her clients to accept. "You're in a trap here," she reminded them. "They have two witnesses and if they both hang tough there's a very good chance you would do jail time. The maximum sentence is five years. In addition, it will obviously be embarrassing to go into detail about the most intimate aspects of your sex life. I think we should take the deal."

Myrna and Gino decided to accept.

For the rest of their lives, they looked upon police and prosecutors as their enemies.

What's Happening Here

Police all over the United States, charged with fighting the war on drugs, have smashed into innocent people's homes repeatedly. Because the police often rely on highly unreliable informants, many of whom are furnishing information in exchange for leniency, they often get the wrong people. In March of 1998, for example, police mistakenly raided the Bronx, New York, apartment of Ellis Elliott. They did not identify themselves as they banged on his front door and Mr. Elliott, believing they were robbers, fired a single pistol shot through the upper part of the doorway. A fusillade of police shooting followed, riddling the apartment with twenty-six bullets. Fortunately, Mr. Elliott was not hit, but he was kicked and beaten by police who repeatedly screamed at him: "Where are the drugs?" An undercover informant had given the wrong address. The police eventually paid for the damages to Mr. Elliott's apartment.

The ACLU's "Freedom Network" reports on a Washington, D.C., case. Police seized the house of a woman whose nephew was suspected of drug dealing. Fifteen FBI agents arrested the nephew, handcuffed the woman, and searched her house, taking TV sets, VCRs, personal papers, and her car. It took twelve officers to tear a built-in TV set out of the wall. One of the policemen was caught on camera saying: "How do you like your new house?"

Sodomy prosecutions are not as rare as they should be either. Like William Fry in the case cited by Regina Middleton in the story (Fry was released from prison in 1990), James David Mosely was imprisoned and tried in Georgia in 1990 for performing cunnilingus on his wife who had accused him of rape, a charge the jury rejected. Georgia was also home to the landmark *Bowers vs. Hardwick* case. Hardwick was convicted of engaging in sodomy with another man. The U.S. Supreme Court upheld his conviction in 1986.

You would think that we could get rid of these arcane laws, many of them dating from the nineteenth century. But few legislators have the courage to vote for their repeal. In Wisconsin in 1990, for instance, state representative Scott Fergus withdrew a bill that would have scrapped Wisconsin's adultery law after talking to a number of his colleagues. "Most of them told me they were very fearful of putting their name on it," he said.

Characterizing the power of government, George Washington said, "It is not eloquence, it is not reason, it is force!" When the government uses force in an effort to control the private behavior of peaceful and otherwise law-abiding citizens, it deprives its citizens of those very rights it is duty-bound to protect. When government becomes a predator based on no greater public purpose than a desire to enforce "moral" behavior, it becomes the enemy of the people and the enemy of liberty.

CHAPTER SEVEN
No Way to Get to Work

Some friends had asked Hugo Tharringer to take them to work in the morning. They agreed to chip in on the gas, and Hugo figured he could pick up some extra money this way. He began taking three men from his block on Philadelphia's Carroll Street to their jobs at a printing plant about a mile away. They caught the bus home. The three passengers paid $1.25 each; they met on the corner of Carroll and Third Avenue at 7:40 every morning, Monday through Friday. The three men were dropped at their plant location fifteen minutes later. With some return passengers added in, Hugo took in an extra twenty-five dollars a week, and he began to see dollar signs in the transportation business.

There must be a lot of people who need transport to their jobs, he figured, people who would be happy to pay a reasonable fee for an exact on-time departure and door-to-door transportation.

Hugo made a deal with his friend Merrill. Merrill had a car and he worked only part-time. To get riders, Hugo contacted friends and friends of friends of his passengers. Then he worked out a route for Merrill and Merrill also began driving, in exchange for fifty percent of the fares.

One fall morning when Hugo arrived at his own passenger pick-up point, a uniformed police officer was waiting.

"We have a report that you're operating a limousine service," he said to Hugo.

"No limousine service. I'm just droppin' these guys off at work."

"Do they pay you for it?"

"They pay some of the gas, that's all," said Hugo.

"If they pay you, then it's a limousine service, and you have to have a license. Do you have a license?"

"No license, no limousine service, no limousine. I'm just droppin' these guys at work. Come on, they're gonna be late."

"I can't help that," said the cop. "I'm giving you a citation for operating a limousine service without a license. You have to appear before an arbitrator at the Department of Transportation next Thursday. You'll have to pay a fine."

"Wait just a minute!" said Hugo. "We're all here trying to make an honest living. We're not breaking any laws. We're minding our own business. Working honestly. Why can't we do it?"

"The law's the law. You can't run a limousine service without a license."

"Can I get a license?"

"You need a vehicle inspection, proof of insurance, documentation that you're not competing with the city buses, stuff like that. I don't know all of it."

"Well, I'm going to take these guys to work, okay?"

"Sorry, buddy. You're operating an illegal limousine service. You're on notice. You can't take paying customers anywhere."

One of Hugo's riders chimed in: "What kind of bullshit is this, man? I got to be at my job in twenty-five minutes. No way I'm going to be there on no damn bus or any other way if I don't get a lift. I don't get to work, I lose my job, I'm on the street. Who are you to tell me I can't go to work?"

"Any more crap out of you, you're going downtown."

Two days later the police confronted and stopped Merrill too. Hugo's fledgling business was dead.

At the hearing, one of Merrill's riders, a middle-aged woman named Hilda, testified at some length.

"I don't know about you," she said to the arbitrator, "but I don't have a choice. If my kids are going to eat, I have to get to work. The bus is no good for me, period. It's late half the time, and I have to change, and even if everything goes okay I'm still half a mile from the building where I work when I get off. I can't afford a taxi, and it's too far to walk, especially if it's raining. So for me there is only one choice. I need somebody to get me every day, without fail, to that job. Merrill's done that every day so far. He's no saint, but he's there every day, 7:30 on the dot. I get to work, I pay $1.25; it works. You take that away from me, you're taking food out of my children's mouths. No transportation, no job."

Also testifying were representatives from the transit authority and from the bus drivers' union. They repeated the law and regulations, that an unlicensed limousine service was unfairly competing with legally established city buses, that the vehicles weren't properly inspected for safety and environmental hazards, and that Hugo's service represented a "rogue element" over which the city exercised no control. It might do anything, like change its route without authority from the city, and it would undermine order and increase traffic.

The arbitrator asked the transit authority man whether he would object to Hugo's service if the vehicles were inspected regularly and passed.

"Still no good," said the transit authority man. "Unlicensed limo services compete directly and undermine established city bus routes. Our drivers have a right to earn a living too. To get a license a limousine has got to prove they're not competing unfairly with the buses, and I know they are. This just shouldn't be allowed."

"Isn't competition healthy?" asked the arbitrator.

"Sure, if it's legal competition," said the transit authority man.

"Well," said the arbitrator, "we're talking about legal transportation here. Suppose Mr. Tharringer had his vehicles inspected, set up some established routes so we'd know where he was driving, and it was legal. Under those circumstances why shouldn't he compete with the buses?"

"Because it's *not* legal. Our drivers have rights. The city buses have been guaranteed the right to these routes. That's the law."

"Logically, I don't buy that argument because it gives the city a monopoly. But you're right about the law."

Hugo lost. The law and its attendant regulations were clear. The licensing requirements were massive, altogether too costly and too complicated for Hugo even to contemplate. And the Transit Authority made it clear that, even if he met all the requirements, they would find a way to turn him down.

What's Happening Here

Many transportation services like Hugo's have been shut down or not allowed to start by government regulations. When government presumes to tell us how we may work, under what conditions, whom we may transport where, government is a job killer. When government imposes restrictions that protect monopolies, particularly government monopolies (which are by far the most difficult to overcome), the government takes away things people need and undermines the public good. Under such circumstances, the government is, surely, the problem, not the solution.

Fortunately, some cases like this have happy outcomes. Leroy Jones's fledgling cab company in Denver, for example, tried repeatedly in the 1990s to get permission to compete with Denver's taxi monopoly. He was turned down by the Colorado Public Utilities Commission, but finally won the right to compete through the court of public opinion. After *Wall Street Journal* editorials and a CBS *Eye On America* segment publicized Jones's desire to operate a taxi in Denver, the bureaucrats backed off. Recognizing the importance of his victory, Jones changed the name of his company from Quick-Pick Cabs to Freedom Cabs. Clint Bolick, an Institute for Justice lawyer who helped bring this about, reports: "Today Freedom Cabs is a thriving enterprise in Denver, operating a fleet of cars and vans and employing dozens of drivers. Meanwhile, following Denver's example, Indianapolis and Cincinnati deregulated their taxicab markets."

But the victories are few and the regulations many, and the regulations inexorably proliferate. Home weavers in New England are forbidden to knit hats and gloves for commercial sale for fear of breaching minimum wage or other such rules. In Charlotte, North Carolina, in 1996, Erma Connell was informed by zoning officials that home-based businesses that produce goods for sale — even pillows and canned jams — are unlawful. In 1997, Linda Fisher, the "muffin lady" of Westminster, Maryland, was ordered to stop selling her home-made muffins, which she delivered on her red-flyer wagon to businesses around town. In her case, as in Leroy Jones's, a media fuss finally produced a solution, but not without a long battle.

In an era when the government is requiring welfare beneficiaries to work or to otherwise move off the welfare rolls, it is particularly destructive that government goes on creating so many barriers to new business enterprises. Transportation services like driving a cab offer excellent opportunities for low-skilled people to get started in a good job. Home-based businesses provide hundreds of thousands of people, especially women, with ways to a better life. Yet the government almost always tries to block such initiatives rather than facilitate them.

How can we expect people at the bottom of the economic ladder to reach the first rung or two if we won't let them?

CHAPTER EIGHT
A Sweet Deal for the Rich

On the ground floor of the Rayburn House Office Building, Congressman Vince Fairweather from the Fifth District of Florida was paying a call on his colleague from North Carolina. "I want your help getting rid of our outdated sugar program," Vince said. "If a Floridian like me can oppose the sugar regime, you can too."

"I don't know," Congressman Barton said. "It has a lot of support. I…."

"But it's insupportable!" Vince said. "The American people pay nearly two billion dollars more than they should for sugar and products that contain it, just so the rich sugar growers can get richer. In my district we've got a lot of single mothers fighting to come off welfare. They're getting minimum wages. They have to support two or three or four people on those wages. The sugar program works against independence for these women, and for men struggling to make it too. They pay more for sugar, for ketchup, for Coke, for virtually any prepared food. And why? It costs more jobs than it maintains. It prevents friendly countries like the Philippines and Brazil from making a living sending sugar here. It's insupportable."

"But we need those Florida districts to hold our majority."

"That's always the argument. We have to have Florida for the elections, so we have to maintain the embargo on Cuba, so we have to maintain the sugar program. You voted to support it last time, didn't you?"

"I'm sorry to say that I did," said Barton. "Nobody complains about it, really. It's just a few pennies more every time people buy something, so they don't really think about it. And you know what Buddy says: 'Poor people shouldn't eat sugar, most of them are too fat anyway.'"

"Buddy's a fool. And he doesn't have any poor constituents. It must be nice to represent a suburban area where everybody makes $50,000."

"Aren't there some environmental angles to this?" Barton asked.

"You bet there are. Runoff from Florida cane fields is polluting the Everglades and taxpayers are footing the bill to clean it up. If we *can* clean it up. There's another issue too. Everyone's concerned about economic stability, more prosperity in the world if we're going to control terrorism. If we won't let our South American neighbors sell us the commodities that produce jobs and hard currency for those countries, how can we expect stability or growth?"

"I'll think about it," Barton said. "It's a pretty rotten program. But we always get pressure from the president, we've got to deliver Florida."

"Think about this too," said Vince. "A major sugar refinery had to be shut down in your pal Ralph Berry's district in Pennsylvania. Sugar's too expensive, so the refineries moved off shore. They just take that business and those jobs and they move to other countries. Candy factories are leaving Chicago for Canada where they can get sugar at world market prices. The American people are not only getting fleeced by the sugar lobby, they're also losing good jobs."

"I'll think about it, I'll think about it," said Barton. "The program may be insupportable, no justification for it. But if nobody's complaining about it, and with growers and the corn sweetener boys making those generous contributions, it's awfully hard to kill."

"It is," said Rogers. "It's harder to kill than a water moccasin in a mangrove tree."

• • •

"I think you'd better speak directly to the President on this one, Raul." Raul's brother Victor had just entered the living room.

"You're probably right," Raul said. "I haven't checked in with the White House for over three months. It's probably time to remind him how hard we're working to hold together Cuban-American support for the elections. Try and nip this Corps of Engineers thing in the bud."

Raul walked up the three polished oak stairs to his study. From behind his desk he could see a half-mile of Florida coastline, a scattering of palm trees, surf gently breaking on a rock and sandy shore. He called the White House, spoke to an aide and arranged a time. Then he swiveled his chair toward the ocean view and pressed a buzzer beneath his desk. In a few minutes, a woman appeared, wearing a black dress and starched white bib apron. She was carrying a tray with a silver coffee pot, steam rising from the spout, a silver pitcher of milk and a large open bowl glistening with large cracked shiny crystals of Florida sugar. "Gracias, Anita."

"De nada, señor."

Twenty-eight minutes later, punctual to the minute, Raul again called the White House and this time was put directly through to the president.

"Good morning, Mr. President," he said. "I want to thank you for your continuing support, for your administration's unwavering stand against the Castro dictatorship. We're behind you, sir. The Cuban-American association is definitely in your corner." A half-minute later Raul got to the main point. "Mr. President, the Corps of Engineers program for the Everglades is a problem. You know that our company and our colleagues in the sugar business are solidly behind reclamation of the Everglades and we will do anything we can to cooperate. But this plan for diverting the water flow goes too far, sir. We'll lose a lot of sugar acreage and that will cost jobs down here, I'm afraid. Perhaps...." Raul was silent for a few minutes, listening. Then he said, "Yes sir. Thank you very much, Mr. President. You know we appreciate it, and we'll back you up. It was good talking to you, sir. My very best regards to Mary."

He pushed another button on his desk and a few minutes later his brother came into the study. "He'll try to help. He said he'd do something. If we can't stop the project, I think we'll at least be able to modify it." Raul paused. "Also, it's time for another contribution. Two hundred thousand, I think. We can top it up later if necessary."

"Does it have to be $200,000? Wouldn't $150,000 be enough?"

"Two hundred thousand. It's an implicit promise."

"Okay."

What's Happening Here

Though there is much competition for this honor, the U.S. sugar program is perhaps the most insupportable and misdirected government subsidy program in existence. It is absolutely regressive, taking from the poor, even those too poor to pay income taxes, to give to the rich. It is anti-trade, freezing out sugar producers in such friendly countries as Brazil, India, and the Philippines from our markets. It perpetuates inefficient agriculture in the U.S., and it is environmentally destructive, encouraging water use practices in Florida that threaten the Everglades.

If anyone were to suggest the creation of such a program today it wouldn't stand a chance. But killing off government programs is practically impossible. As Milton Friedman has pointed out, when the benefits of a program are highly concentrated and visible to a small number of people, and the costs of the program are diffuse and nearly invisible to those who have to pay, the political processes always work in favor of the special-interest beneficiaries. Such groups are willing to spend vast amounts of time and treasure to keep their lucrative privileges flowing.

The U.S. Office of Budget and Management estimates that the American people are paying $1.8 billion too much for food every year because the current program inflates the price of sugar. It does so by strictly limiting the amount of sugar that can be imported into the United States, by providing concessional loans to sugar producers here, and by guaranteeing prices to sugar growers that are way above world market prices.

The program is a complex component of the dysfunctional farm price support scheme, which is lavishly maintained for dairy products, sugar, peanuts, cotton, rice, soybeans, wheat, and other staples. In 2002 Congress passed, and the president signed the largest agricultural subsidy program in the nation's history. It will cost taxpayers $180 billion over ten years.

This policy does not protect the person you or I think of as a farmer, notes Tom Buis of the National Farmers Union. "It benefits the largest operations and the processors." The *New York Times'* Tom Weiner confirms what everyone involved in these programs knows: "Federal farm policy is creating bigger and bigger farms and fewer and fewer farmers."

The sugar program has made centi-millionaires of several sugar growers in Florida, and they have shown their gratitude. Florida sugar interests have contributed millions to the political campaigns of both parties and the money continues to flow.

Meanwhile, mothers struggling to get off welfare, ordinary Americans working hard to get by, and two-income families just making ends meet all continue chipping in to make the sugar barons even richer.

CHAPTER NINE
At the Mercy of Airbags

Julia was gazing out at her garden one sunny afternoon when her friend Heloise knocked at the front door. Since Heloise dropped by regularly on Thursday afternoons, Julia was not surprised at her arrival. They were soon seated and having tea on the back porch. The sun was shining and a half-dozen black-capped chickadees chirped in the maple trees. Heloise was telling Julia about a radio program she'd heard that morning on the subject of airbags.

"I think this will interest you, Julia. They were discussing airbags in cars and they said that if you have children or small adults riding in the front seat, having airbags is more dangerous than no airbags. By exploding, airbags can save lives because they cushion the impact, but they can also injure people when they explode. The government expert on the program said airbags are usually more dangerous than helpful for all children in the front seat and also for adults who are very short, particularly if they're slim. I've always envied you for wearing a size six, but you may want to consider having your airbag disconnected."

"Are you sure about this?" Julia asked. "For small people the airbag actually increases the danger?"

"The man on the radio seemed very certain. If you weigh less than 100 pounds, there's a serious risk."

"I will definitely look into it," Julia said.

Two weeks later, Julia and Heloise met for tea again. This time the chickadees were chirping but the sun was behind a stubbornly large grey cloud and the air on the back porch was brisk.

"I've looked into the airbag matter, Heloise," Julia said. "You're right that a driver-side airbag is more a menace than a help for people like me. But it turns out that I'm not permitted to disconnect my own airbag, or to have it disconnected. Garages and car dealers aren't allowed to disconnect it — it's against the law!

"However, the government has instituted a system so that mechanics and dealers are permitted to disconnect airbags under certain circumstances. There's a government brochure — here's a copy — called Airbag On-Off Switches: Questions and Answers."

Julia sighed and pulled her cardigan sweater more closely around her shoulders. Then she began reading from the brochure. "'Under the exemption,' — by 'exemption' they mean the rule that exempts people like me from having to live with this danger; it gets clear in a minute." Then she went back to reading aloud from the brochure. "'Under the exemption, vehicle owners may request a retrofit on-off switch, based on informed decision-making and their certification of their membership or the membership of another user of their vehicle in one of the risk groups identified by the agency.' I've never thought of myself as being a member of a 'risk group,' but the government thinks I am. The brochure also includes among these risk groups 'individuals who cannot position themselves with the center of their breastbone at least ten inches back from the center of the driver airbag cover.' I've made measurements, including measurements with another person in the car watching me, and in fact I do drive with the center of my chest less than ten inches from the airbag cover. I can't drive any other way.

"But in order to get permission to have my garage mechanic disconnect the airbag, the federal government requires me to submit a form. Here it is — 'Form OMB No. 2127-0588, Request for Airbag On-Off Switch.'"

"This is really too much, Julia. Why don't they just let you have it disconnected?"

"Well, they do, but you have to use the form. With this OMB form, I can certify that I belong to an approved 'risk group,' and I also certify that I've read this other government brochure called 'Airbags and On-Off Switches, Information for an Informed Decision.' Of course the government is aware that people who might want to disconnect their airbags for frivolous or purely personal reasons could fill out this form with something other than the truth. They therefore remind us, right on the form, that false statements may result in 'criminal prosecution under Title 18, United States Code, Section 1001.' There's always a threat in it with the government. So I was very careful in filling out this form."

"Well," said Heloise, "It's an unbelievable amount of trouble, and I understand your being upset about all of it, but at least you'll be able to disconnect your airbag now and you'll be safer."

"I'm afraid not, Heloise," Julia said. "My mechanic says he won't accept the authorization letter, even when I receive it and present it to him. He says there are too many legal risks involved in disconnecting an airbag, that there are so many regulations about all this that he might be sued by the owner of any car whose airbag he disconnects if there's trouble in the future, and so he won't do it. I checked with the garage in Brighton too. They say the same thing."

"But how can that be? If the government's decided it's safer for you to be without an airbag, and provides you with a letter authorizing the mechanic to disconnect it, how can he refuse?"

"He says he'll be sued. And I don't believe he can be made to do anything he doesn't want to do. It looks like I'll just have to go on living with an unnecessary menace in my life."

What's Happening Here

The idea that the citizens of a free country should have to beg the government for the right to do whatever they wish to do to their own automobiles if it poses no risks to others is very troubling indeed. Not only is it impossible to buy a new vehicle without an airbag in the United States today, but disconnecting airbags is not a legal option unless you are either a member of a "risk group" or pretend to be. The tangled thicket of regulations, well intended as usual, has created a nightmarish mess. As of November 1, 1997, 87 people, 38 adults and 49 children, had been killed by exploding airbags. While this was just a fraction of those estimated to have been saved by airbags, there is no question that people who feel themselves at risk ought to be able to do what they consider in their own best interests.

By mid-1998, the National Highway Traffic Safety Administration, which administers this regulatory thicket, had issued more than 30,000 authorization letters for the disconnection of airbags by installing on-off switches; it had received back only 1,000 acknowledgements from mechanics, who are obliged to submit the NHTSA acknowledgement form within seven days after installing such on-off switches. Meanwhile, the recipients of the letters were complaining long and hard that garages and dealers would not honor the authorization letters because of the incomprehensibility of the regulations and their fears of litigation.

Instead of playing nanny, the government should allow people to make their own decisions about disconnecting or keeping airbags in their own cars, without any paperwork whatsoever.

CHAPTER TEN
Losing the Kids after "Adultery"

Brian's fiftieth birthday had been, ostensibly, a success. Two of Brian's college classmates had showed up unexpectedly and they and their wives had pitched in with the party preparations.

In the midst of what Brian's wife, Jillian, was coming to believe were excessively fussy arrangements, she had realized that she was tired of the whole business. She was tired of Brian's birthdays, which were celebrated with more fanfare than her own; she was tired of buying his socks and underwear; she was tired of his dependence on her.

Yes, she had known what she was getting into when she married Brian eight years before. She knew he was looking for a woman to take care of him as well as his children. His mother had devoted her life to "taking care" of her husband, and it was clear that Brian expected similar treatment. But it was just too much. He didn't even know his own shirt size! She operated the checking account, ran the house, and got very little in return.

Brian had come to the marriage with two children because the children's mother had had a nervous breakdown when she and Brian separated, and she was all too willing to turn over custody to Brian and his new, very competent wife. So raising Angie and Paul — ages three and five — had fallen on Jillian's shoulders, while, at the same time, she was expected to be a virtual mother to her husband. Except for the kids, she was tired of it.

After the guests had gone home, Brian lay down in front of the fireplace and asked her to rub his back, something she had always done on special occasions. This time her hands rebelled. She went through the motions, but she rubbed with the heels of her hands; she couldn't bring herself to use her fingertips. That touch was too intimate for someone she was coming to despise.

Sex was another matter. Jillian was perfectly capable of sex without intimacy. So when Brian slid his hand between her legs as she straddled him for the backrub, she let him fondle and stimulate her to climax. But this would be the last time.

A week later she suggested to Brian that he should move out. He was stunned. "What about the kids?" he asked.

"The kids can stay with me. You know they depend on me. We'll work out the custody details later." Reeling, Brian told Paul and Angie that he was going on a business trip and that he would return in ten days, two weeks at the most.

When he got back two weeks later, Paul and Angie seemed completely happy, completely normal. In the context of his failing marriage, Brian was especially moved to see his children, and realized that he could never give them up. Jillian had been the only mother they had known for the past eight years and she had certainly been more of a parent than he. But Paul, especially, filled an emotional void in Brian's life; Brian's heart went out to the boy who was beginning to experience the fears and uncertainties of adolescence, and to Angie, too. He could never accept an arrangement that granted custody of his children to Jillian.

On the other hand, he didn't know what to do.

Five days after Brian's return Jillian sent Paul and Angie to their aunt's, three houses down the block, and she confronted Brian. "The kids are happy. The kids are fine with me. There's no need to make a change."

"I'm sorry, Jillian. I accept that our marriage has failed. I accept that you no longer want to look after my needs. I'll have to find someone else to do that. But Paul and Angie are my children. They must come with me. I'll make a good home for them. I'll find them another person, another woman, to fill that role."

"No you won't," said Jillian. "I've raised those two since they were tiny. They both call me Mother. For all practical purposes I am their mother. That's the end of it, Brian. I think you know better than to fight me on something like this."

"I won't fight you, or rather this is not between you and me. My children need me, and I need them. And they are my children. That's a fact."

"They need *me*! If there's a fight you know I'll win it." Brian got up, walked slowly out of the room, and left the house.

Three months later there was a hearing before a judge. Brian and Jillian were there, represented by lawyers. The judge reviewed the facts: "As I understand it, the facts are not contested here. Paul, age thirteen, and Angie, age eleven, are the biological children of Brian Scofield, who is here today, and his first wife, Virginia Scofield, who has been notified of this proceeding and who has chosen to make no representation. The children have been in the custody of Mr. Scofield and his wife of eight years, Jillian Scofield...."

Jillian's lawyer interrupted: "Jillian Baxter, your honor. Ms. Baxter has resumed her maiden name."

"Jillian Baxter. This is a preliminary hearing to determine issues relating to the custody of the two children. Mr. Scofield asserts his rights as biological father of the children and their guardian since their birth. Ms. Baxter asserts a claim for custody based on having served in the general place and function of the mother to these children over the past eight years. Is that correct?" Both lawyers nodded.

"There is always, of course, a strong presumption in favor of biological parents. There is often, too, a presumption in favor of the mother, who may have been more active in the child-rearing capacity. In this case, the biological mother is not in the picture, so the presumption would normally go to the biological father. However, the facts of this case are unusual and I wish to study the matter further. I will let you know."

Jillian and her lawyer huddled in his offices following the hearing. "It doesn't look very promising," he said to her.

"Isn't there something we can do here?" Jillian asked. "There's got to be some way to put pressure on him."

"Well, it's a long shot, of course, but there is always adultery."

"What do you mean?" Jillian said.

"Well, in trying to convince the judge that he could provide a good home for his kids, Brian admitted on the record that he was living with his new girlfriend. You and he are still married. That's adultery. It's a felony in this state. The law is practically never enforced, but it's still the law. If we could get the DA to charge him with felony adultery, it would put some real pressure on him and he might bend."

"If he was convicted of a crime, might that affect the judge's decision?" Jillian asked.

"It might. It might not. But it would certainly give us some leverage."

"Who's the DA now? Is it still Jake MacIntire?"

"Yes. Jake's been DA for over a decade. Pretty tough prosecutor. He might not go for an adultery prosecution. He generally focuses on serious crime. Still, it's possible...."

"I know Jake. Maybe I'll give it a try," Jillian said. In fact Jillian had dated Jake MacIntire several times during their senior year in high school and they had met on a few occasions after Jillian had gone away to college. She had been, she thought, well, accommodating with Jake. He owed her one.

"It's been quite a while," Jake said, when she called at the District Attorney's office in the basement of the courthouse building.

"It has, Jake. How have you been?" They exchanged pleasantries and Jillian got down to the point. "I know you don't normally prosecute adultery cases," she said. "But this is an extraordinary case. My husband has abandoned me, and abandoned his own children whom I have raised, and he has moved in with another woman, probably someone he's been seeing for a long time. It's exactly the kind of behavior the adultery law was meant to condemn and prevent. I'm asking you to prosecute him."

"I wouldn't prosecute an adultery case. The community wouldn't stand for an investigation of people's sexual habits," Jake said.

"You don't have to do that. He's admitted in court that he's cohabiting with Florence. It's on the record. The judge asked him specifically whether he was representing to the Court that he and Florence Mattigan were cohabiting. Brian said that they were. He gave that as an argument as to why he should have custody of the children."

"You sure it's in the public record?"

"Absolutely sure."

"Well, it is the law. Tell you what. I'll do a little research, see what the law says exactly and what the precedents are in this jurisdiction. And I'll check the court record and see exactly what he said and what the judge asked. If it's an open-and-shut case, and if he's abandoned you as you say, maybe I'll do it. Might even earn me some points with the blue-noses, who knows?"

• • •

"You've been indicted," Marsha McCurdy said to Brian. Marsha McCurdy was Brian's attorney, and she was steaming mad. "This is the only adultery prosecution in this state for more than fifty years. Yes, it's a felony. If the aggrieved spouse makes a formal complaint, and your wife apparently did, the law is there and it can be enforced. This is idiotic, of course. Nobody expects the adultery laws to be enforced, and they practically never are. But in this situation it could really hurt you. If you're a convicted felon, your wife, soon to be your ex-wife, can make a much stronger case that you are an unfit parent for your own children. I don't think Judge Greenfield would take such a conviction seriously, but it is a felony, and it does have to be weighed into the balance. This gives them considerably more leverage."

"I don't believe it," Brian said. "I don't believe she can actually get me this way. She's trying to turn me into a criminal."

"It won't go to trial, anyway. This is obviously meant for a plea bargain, for working out some kind of a deal. But she's really screwed you over. This could cost you custody. I hope not, but it could."

At a long afternoon conference in Judge Greenfield's chambers, attended by the Assistant District Attorney and by Jillian's and Brian's lawyers, it was clear that the adultery conviction was a foregone conclusion and that Judge Greenfield would consider the felony count to weigh seriously in the balance of the custody equation. Marsha had to backpedal, fighting for everything. She managed to get reasonable visitation rights, but custody of his own children was out of the question for Brian. Wednesday afternoons and alternate weekends was the best she could do.

What's Happening Here

Legislators pass laws they don't expect will be enforced. They shouldn't. Such legislative activity constitutes one of the best illustrations of why Winston Churchill described democracy as the worst form of government except for all the others.

Americans seem opposed to divorce in principle, but practically no one opposes Uncle Joe's or sister Sally's divorce. Uncle Joe and sister Sally made the right decision. We know them and their marriages weren't working. Similarly, we tend to be opposed to adultery, gambling, and prostitution, but most of the time we don't want the government to actually get involved in such matters.

An adultery prosecution much like Brian's was brought in Wisconsin in 1990. "The law's on the books," the District Attorney said. "For me to decide not to prosecute would be, in effect, to declare the statute null and void." So he pressed charges against twenty-eight-year-old Donna Carroll because, he said, Wisconsin has a substantial interest in preventing adultery to support "the stability and best interests of marriage and the family." Other adultery prosecutions have been recently brought in Alabama and Massachusetts.

In 1990, a number of district attorneys in Connecticut were persuaded by irate husbands and wives in divorce proceedings to bring criminal adultery charges against their estranged spouses. The Connecticut legislature was so appalled by the enforcement of this statute that they promptly repealed Connecticut's adultery law, and the governor was happy to go along.

Laws governing our private sexual behavior are clearly dysfunctional. They are enforced because prosecutors are out to get somebody, because of political or personal influence, or for other reasons having little to do with the administration of justice. The principal consequence of such laws is discriminatory attacks on people like Brian in circumstances where fairness and the interests of children are difficult enough to assess without the added legal and emotional freight of a criminal prosecution.

CHAPTER ELEVEN
Roger and the Nicotine Wars

"I see an opportunity, a golden opportunity," Grigori said to Sam Masters. Sam was a short, stocky man who had been Grigori's assistant for sixteen years. "I believe this opportunity will last and last."

Grigori's office was on the twenty-first floor of a high-rise building in a medium-rent area of downtown Atlanta, Georgia. Grigori was an importer and a shipper. He had made a living for many years hauling goods around the world. Some of those goods, as he knew, were unloaded in the middle of the night and found their way past customs officials who could sometimes be fooled and who could more often be bribed. Grigori also knew that high tariffs were a lucrative source of income for a variety of people as well as the governments that imposed them. He did not mind being one of the beneficiaries.

"What's the opportunity, boss?" Sam said.

"The opportunity, Sam, the golden opportunity, is cigarettes. Full-nicotine cigarettes. From Europe, from the Far East, even from Canada."

"What's wrong with American cigarettes?"

"What's wrong with American cigarettes, Sam, is the FDA. This year the nicotine content of cigarettes in the United States will be reduced by ten percent. That's not much and probably not very many people will notice. But next year it will be reduced by another ten percent, and another ten percent every year after that until the nicotine content is less than half of what it was last year. That's the law. Congress gave the Food and Drug Administration the authority to control tobacco, and this is what the FDA has decided to do, bless their hearts."

"So?" said Sam, who liked to have things explained very clearly.

"So every year there will be more and more people who want full-nicotine cigarettes and will pay a premium price to get them. Every year there will be a bigger and bigger demand for Gauloises from France, for Passport cigarettes from Malaysia, for Wills from India, and for Benson & Hedges, because the Marlboro man is going limp. Camels and Marlboros and Winstons will be getting weak and feeble. Smokers will be sucking on them until they're blue in the face and not getting what they need. They'll pay ten or even twenty dollars a pack for real cigarettes. That's the golden opportunity. Real cigarettes will be illegal, but they'll be available all over the world outside of the US of A. They'll get mark-ups of 1,000 percent, just like cocaine and marijuana.

"Illegal means profitable. Illegal means the prices go way, way up. Illegal means we've got a whole new category of cargo, cargo we can get double and triple rates for. Let us give thanks to the Congress of the United States for giving the FDA control over nicotine."

"I see," said Sam.

"I'm already under way with our friends at Bertha's Bakery."

"I like their mini-pies," Sam said.

"Never mind the pies," Grigori said. "They're experts at hauling hot cargo."

• • •

A little over two years after Grigori and Sam's conversation, Roger Feldman backed his semi carefully into the loading dock of a building supply distributor. Roger was a long-haul driver who owned his own eighteen-wheeler. He transported everything from books to vegetables to teddy bears over thousands of miles of interstate and made a pretty good living at it. He occasionally wondered whether some of the thousands of cases and crates he carried might contain things that shouldn't be there, but he had no certain knowledge that this was so and he didn't spend a lot of time worrying about it.

Cigarettes were a regular cargo for Roger. He liked hauling cigarettes. The cigarette cases were bulky, but they didn't weigh much and they were clean. Roger didn't have to scrub his truck out after hauling cigarettes.

Today Roger was hauling plumbing fixtures. A man he hadn't seen before walked up. "I understand you're making a run to St. Louis?"

"That's right," Roger said.

"My name's Sam. Sam Masters. You want to haul some cigarettes to St. Louie?"

"How many? How much?"

"Twenty cases. Two thousand."

He'd have to make room for the cigarettes, but two thousand dollars was a nice fat overpayment.

"Sure," Roger said. "That works."

Roger especially liked St. Louis runs. His girlfriend lived there and he had reached the age where he really liked to see her as often as possible, and no one else. Her name was

Elvira and she taught American history to sixth and seventh graders. She was two years older than Roger, almost exactly as tall and broad-shouldered, a large woman but not over-weight. Roger liked everything about her, including her wide hips and heavy breasts, but he didn't like the fact that she smoked. Roger had given up smoking when he was twenty-nine, and he didn't like the taste of it on her breath. But, he figured, if that was her only fault, he would put up with it.

On his last St. Louis trip he'd taken her a present. When he arrived at her apartment, they had their "ten-second kiss," as they always did. Elvira had read in one of those relationship books that couples should kiss for ten seconds at least twice a day when they were around each other, so Roger was used to getting his ten-second taste of cigarettes, along with the good tastes of Elvira's lips. He had brought her something he knew she would like, Malaysian Marlboros.

"Hey!" she had said, hugging him. "I've never had those. Kelly says they're terrific. Almost as good as Marlboros used to be back in the twentieth century. Gimme!" Roger had handed over two cartons.

Today's St. Louis run started with a pickup of building supplies — plumbing fixtures mostly — then garden tools, seeds, and fertilizers that would fill about three-quarters of his truck. He'd cancelled a small consignment of conven-ience store items to make room for the cigarettes, which would be added later. Sam Masters had given him a map that showed a rendezvous point a few miles south of the city, at a freeway rest stop where he would meet up with an outsized panel truck with "Bertha's Bakery" stenciled on both sides. The cases of cigarettes would be marked "Winston" but these Winstons were made in India, 100 percent nicotine, 100 per-cent illegal.

After a frustrating half hour on the crowded interstate Roger pulled his semi into a truck slot at the rest stop. He immediately spotted the Bertha's Bakery van. Next to it was a police car with rotary lights flashing. One state trooper had his polished boot on the van's bumper and was filling out a report. Another spoke into a radio. Roger looked the other way, then walked casually to the men's room and unzipped at the urinal. "What happened?" he said off-handedly to the man standing next to him.

"Murder. Looks like a cigarette smuggling case. Cops say they found the driver dead a little while ago. A nicotine killing."

What's Happening Here

When the government outlaws something that people want, the black market takes over. That means higher prices, huge profits, police corruption, and murder. This is an immutable law, which governments seem unable to grasp.

CHAPTER TWELVE
Dueling Disabilities

Rodrigo was blind, and he was spitting mad. For the third time this morning he heard the screech of car wheels near him coming to a sudden stop, and he knew it was his fault. He couldn't find the curb anymore! The wheelies, the goddamn wheelies had taken over the ADA — the Americans with Disabilities Act. Those guys in the wheelchairs had gotten the machinery of the law under their control. When they made curbs wheelchair-accessible, did they consult the blind? Of course not! They just scooped out those curbs, so I can never find them, so I don't know when I'm wandering off the sidewalk onto the street. This'll probably get me killed!

What's Happening Here

The Americans with Disabilities Act, signed into law in 1990, is a well-intentioned federal effort to make places of public access and the workplace more usable for Americans with disabilities. But, as with all laws, there ensued a myriad of unforeseen consequences. A Wendy's restaurant divisional maintenance manager, for example, took some pride in making the entrances to ninety-seven Wendy's restaurants easily accessible to people in wheelchairs. He went an accommodating step further and marked two tables near the door with the stylized wheelchair symbols for disabled customers. He was chagrined to be accused, by several representatives of disabled groups, of creating a "disabled ghetto." "Get a grip," remarked columnist William Raspberry about the wheelchair-bound complainers who apparently felt offended.

A more serious problem with the ADA is that the definition of disability is being expanded to include psychological problems and conditions difficult to distinguish from "normal." For example, severe obesity is categorized as a disability, while excessive weight is not. Thus, people who are grossly overweight can demand rights of their employers that people who are very much overweight cannot.

Worse, the ADA does not seem to have helped more disabled people get hired. Early analysis by the National Organization of the Disabled showed thirty-one percent of working-age disabled persons employed in 1993, compared to thirty-three percent in 1986, before the law took effect. Fear of lawsuits is probably the reason. Of the roughly 15,000 ADA complaints filed annually, ninety percent are by people already employed.

Most employers accommodate talented employees regardless of their disabilities. But codifying these matters into law leads to more compulsory structuring of society, less flexibility about individual circumstances, and a general lowering of civil discourse and decency.

CHAPTER THIRTEEN
The Charge Is "Conspiracy"

Luisa had been dancing continuously for almost forty minutes, dancing hard. The music and a second glass of Chardonnay were getting into her blood. Her boyfriend, Carl, seemed to be dancing with every other woman at the party.

The music stopped. "Break time," said Luisa. She was dancing with Greg, a man she had met a few weeks before at a party at Carl's apartment. Greg was good looking and he seemed friendly, but he was square. Luisa couldn't decide if he was an interesting square or a genuine, gold-plated doofus. His suit looked like Brooks Brothers and his collar was, literally, buttoned down. Why not something casual or maybe Armani? Luisa wondered. Anything but Brooks Bros! Still, he was handsome and a very good dancer and he was good friends with Carl. That counted for a lot.

"A break sounds good to me," Greg said. "I'll be downstairs."

When Luisa got back to the dance room, the music was throbbing again and Carl came toward her, moving carefully, his double-breasted jacket slung over his right shoulder. "Want to do a line?" he asked, his mouth next to her ear.

"Sure, why not? I mean, are you sure it's safe?"

"It's safe enough," said Carl. "We'll use Alice's bathroom next to where the coats are."

Twenty minutes later, Luisa was feeling very good. "I want to dance!" she said to Carl.

"Not me," he said. "I want to go with this. I want to float through it. Dancing would spoil it."

Luisa looked for Greg. Maybe he was square but he danced the way she wanted to dance now; loose, fluid, sexy. She found him and grabbed his shirt under the armpits on both sides and gently shook him back and forth. "Let's dance! I'm going to float right over the dance floor and you're going to float with me."

"Whoa. What are you on?"

"Never mind what I'm on. I want to dance!"

After a few minutes the music slowed. "Tell me what you're on. I'm curious," Greg said.

"Never mind, never mind. No big deal, just a little line. Just a little fun."

"You get it from Carl?"

"Never mind. We just get it, that's all." She paused. "You're a good dancer," she said. "You look square with your Lands' End button-down, but you dance real loose, nice. How long have you known Carl?"

"Oh, Carl and I go way back. We were going to be roommates in college. Then he decided to rush one of the fraternities and I stayed in the dorm. But we're good friends. We go back."

They danced for a few more minutes without speaking, the rhythm and the percussive throb of the music seeming louder, matching Luisa's movements and the beat of blood in her veins. She was above the dance floor, she could see down from a long way away, see people's heads from way up somewhere, their arms moving slowly, like wings, like a flock of geese, like a flying wedge, like icebergs floating oh-so-slowly in a river.

When the music slowed again Greg said, "I wonder where Carl gets his stuff? It must be pretty good stuff."

"Oh yes, it's good. It's good. Alonzo's got the best. Alonzo's a brick, he's my pal."

"Alonzo who?"

"Listen to Mr. Curious! Why? You don't do coke, do you? Carl says you don't even drink. Is that right?"

"Well usually that's right. But you never know." He was silent for a minute. "Have you known Alonzo for long?"

"I've known him for a while. He's a nice guy. You should ask Carl about Alonzo. All I know is that he has good stuff. We got some extra last...."

"What?"

"Never mind."

Luisa had caught herself too late. Greg's contacts at the police department had been building a dossier on Alonzo Pritchard for some time, and they had also been building a case on Carl. With Luisa's corroboration of these connections and at least partial corroboration of a sale, the DA stepped up the investigation and, on a frosty February night, three members of the narcotics squad smashed in the door of Alonzo's apartment. They found nearly half a kilogram of powdered cocaine, arrested Alonzo, and began pressuring him to "cooperate." They wanted him to give them Carl and Luisa.

Alonzo was easy. As a third-time drug offender, he was facing a possible life sentence, and he was ready to give the police anything they wanted in exchange for more lenient treatment. He confirmed that Carl had visited his apartment for the purpose of purchasing cocaine and he swore that he had looked out his apartment window when Carl left and had seen Luisa driving the car. He understood that the investigators wanted more, so he added that Carl was converting some of the powdered cocaine into crack, that Carl had told him this, and there was another prisoner in the jail where he had been held who could confirm this as an eyewitness. The "eyewitness," also desperate for leniency, willingly lied about the crack, and the police had their case. Carl and Luisa were indicted for possession of cocaine with intent to sell.

Through a friend, Luisa found a lawyer, Jimmy Harper. He accompanied Luisa to the arraignment, where she was formally charged and photographed and fingerprinted. "I don't understand what's going on," she said to Jimmy. "I haven't bought or sold any cocaine. I've never been involved in a sale. Yeah, I've used it a few times, but what is this 'conspiracy' business? I didn't conspire to do anything. I just sniffed a little coke."

"You don't have to actually buy and sell to be convicted of conspiracy," Jimmy told her. "If you were involved in the transaction even in an indirect way, like driving a car to bring Carl to Alonzo's, and you knew what the trip was for, that's 'conspiracy.' It's bad. Now that Alonzo's given them testimony about converting the cocaine powder to crack, it's ten times worse. The penalties for crack are much higher. It doesn't matter that it's a lie; I think the prosecutor probably knows it's a lie, but he wants convictions one way or another and he's going to get them."

"That's crazy! Crack's dangerous! I would never have anything to do with crack. Neither would Carl. How can they say that?"

"The reason Alonzo can say it is that he's facing a life sentence and he'll say anything. What would you do if this was the only way out of spending your life in prison? And they can make it stick because the police and the prosecutor want to believe it; because it gives them more leverage over you and over Carl." He stopped and put out his hand, just touching her shoulder. "You're in deep trouble, Luisa. You're facing a minimum of ten years in the penitentiary. You knew about the mandatory minimum sentences, didn't you?" He sighed. "How could you get into this?"

"We were just doing a little line! It didn't do me any harm, and it didn't do anyone else any harm." She was crying now.

Jimmy Harper sympathized. "It's easy to forget how harsh these laws are. The sentences, even for nonviolent first offenders, are horrendous."

"But I wasn't hurting anybody. Why should other people care what I put in my body? I'm the only one who can decide about that."

"All that's irrelevant. The drug laws are insane, but they're laws." He rubbed his temples with his fingertips. "Let's see what we can salvage from this."

Among other things, Jimmy was concerned about his fee. He couldn't afford to take Luisa's case pro bono. His client didn't qualify as poor, but she was badly strapped for cash, and if she went to jail she would lose the income from her job. Jimmy agreed to defer payment of most of his fee against the anticipated alimony and child support being paid Luisa by her ex-husband; those payments so far had been regular. But even if they kept coming, Jimmy knew he was taking a big risk. With his client in jail, the money from the ex-husband might be used up paying for Luisa's daughter's necessities. The little girl, Melanie, was in kindergarten and, from what Jimmy could learn, she would have to live with an aunt or her grandmother if her mother was incarcerated. Her father lived in Tokyo and said he did not have a home appropriate for raising a child.

Jimmy had a long talk with the prosecutor and heard what he expected: The U.S. Attorney's office would go for the mandatory minimum for Luisa — ten years for a first offense. The assistant U.S. Attorney claimed he had a strong case against Luisa for conspiracy. She had driven the car, more than 300 grams were involved, and the crack testimony cinched it. Luisa's only hope, he said, was to provide testimony on all drug dealings and activities of which she had knowledge, starting with Carl. Then she might get a "5K-1" reduction in her sentence.

Jimmy was not surprised by this. He knew that real dealers — the men (they usually were men) who actually made the big money dealing drugs — were seldom sent away for more than a few years at a time. They cooperated with prosecutors by fingering other parties in the drug trade, often testifying against them at trial; this willingness to snitch nearly always resulted in a dramatic decrease in the length of their sentences. But women accomplices in these "conspiracies" often got the full sentence because they had less evidence to give or refused to testify against their boyfriends.

Luisa knew about some of Carl's transactions, and now she understood that that knowledge was her best chance for leniency. If she testified against Carl, the state would have an airtight case against him and could use that leverage to get his evidence on Alonzo and the others. Jimmy proposed this to Luisa.

"Absolutely not. I will not talk about Carl."

"What if he snitches on you? He may, you know. In these cases it's very common for the man to testify against the woman, even when he was the one who initiated the transaction, procured the stuff, and did most of the crime."

"I don't care. I don't think he'll testify against me," said Luisa. "But even if he does, I won't testify against him. It would be betraying everything I believe in. If we aren't loyal to the people we're close to, life isn't worth living. No deal. I refuse, absolutely, to snitch on Carl. I won't do it."

"You may do a long time in jail, then. I mean it, Luisa. Testifying against Carl could make the difference between ten years in the penitentiary and maybe just three or four. Think about it. For Melanie the difference is a lifetime — ten years without her mother means growing up with you in jail. You've got to think about it."

Luisa thought long and hard, especially about Melanie, and first grade and fifth grade and graduating to junior high. She thought about Melanie in high school editing the school paper or being first in her science class or best in Spanish. And Melanie would meet boys and go for advice to Luisa's mother, and to Luisa's sister, but not to her. As she thought about all this, Luisa couldn't keep from crying, crying this time for Melanie.

But she still couldn't turn state's evidence on Carl. She loved him, or she had loved him, and the words would stick in her throat when she even thought of uttering them. When she pictured herself on the witness stand or signing a declaration, she knew she just couldn't do it.

In long meetings with Jimmy, she agonized over whether to plead and accept the mercy of the Court, which she understood was limited by laws requiring a mandatory minimum sentence, or insist upon a trial by a jury. Jimmy knew that Luisa couldn't really afford the expense of a trial, not if he was going to get paid for his time, and this had to be weighed in the balance.

They finally decided on a compromise. They would go to trial, but spend as little as possible. The trial would probably last only a day or two. Luisa clung to the hope that at least a few of the jurors would be sympathetic to the fact that she was the mother of a five-year-old girl. She hoped they might find her not guilty for that reason. Jimmy told her that by law the jury couldn't base a decision on this reasoning, but jurors sometimes did that kind of thing anyway. He would do his best to cast a reasonable doubt on her involvement with the actual selling of the cocaine and its use for making crack. If the jury could be convinced that she hadn't known about the crack angle, and that she had never sold, or intended to sell any drugs, her sentence might be shortened.

Their hopes were in vain. The jury found Luisa guilty of conspiracy to possess cocaine with intent to sell. At her sentencing two weeks later, the judge said: "With a guilty verdict in your case, I have absolutely no choice. For a federal conspiracy conviction, there is an immovable mandatory minimum sentence of ten years for the first offense, even if, as in your case, there is no prior record of any criminal activity. The only way to shorten your sentence is by recommendation from the prosecutor on the grounds that you have cooperated with the prosecution, and I have no such recommendation.

"With great regret, I sentence you to ten years confinement at the Cruickshank Women's Penitentiary, with no possibility of parole."

What's Happening Here

Thousands of women like Luisa, who "drove the car," or were "in the room," in connection with a drug purchase have then been convicted of conspiracy to use/buy/sell drugs. Our jails are filled with such people, people who, for the most part, have done nothing to harm anyone else.

Under Michigan's "650 Lifer" law, JeDonna Young, whose boyfriend was involved in drug dealing, was sentenced to life imprisonment in 1978. She served more than twenty years, watching the two-year-old son she left behind mature into a grown man. "JeDonna has been a model prisoner," Families Against Mandatory Minimums reported, "earning a college degree and becoming a certified paralegal who screens clients for prison legal services of Michigan." She was finally paroled in 1999.

Gloria L. VanWinkle, a middle-class mother of two and a cocaine addict, is today serving a life sentence in the maximum-security unit at the state prison for women in Topeka, Kansas. She was convicted of possession of forty dollars worth of cocaine, her third possession offense, in 1992. Her children, ages nine and thirteen, were still visiting her regularly as this book went to press.

The *Boston Globe* reports that eight out of every ten drug offenders in Massachusetts prisons are serving an average sentence of about five years for their first offense, nearly one year longer than the average state sentence for a rape or assault. For the most part, they are first-time offenders, drug users at the bottom of the supply chain, not the big-time dealers the mandatory sentencing laws were intended to catch. Massachusetts Superior Court Judge Robert Barkin told the *Globe* that, though presiding over a criminal court for twenty years, "I have never had a really top dealer before me. Invariably they are street dealers or mules who end up taking up jail space. Most do more time than those who commit crimes of violence against another person."

The war on drugs not only has filled America's jails with nonviolent "criminals," it has also corrupted our police, undermined the political and jurisprudential systems of many other nations, including our closest neighbors in Latin America, caused a sharp rise and continuing high level of homicides, and multiplied other crimes as drug users seek to pay for their habits, which are made shockingly expensive by our laws. The drug war has made international kingpins of men who would otherwise be petty criminals and who now control empires worth hundreds of millions of dollars.

With few and isolated exceptions, the use of drugs does not cause real crime. The violence that attends the drug war is almost entirely the result of the criminalization of drugs, not their use.

Yet otherwise enlightened members of Congress continue to posture and maintain that we must not "give up" on the war on drugs. Why? Since the earliest days of the human species, people have chosen to use mind- and mood-altering substances. Alcohol is probably the most common, and its negative effects are substantial. Yet we have found that the costs of outlawing alcohol far outweigh the dangers of keeping it legal. One of the most deadly substances in the United States — ordinary tobacco — kills an estimated 400,000 persons every year, a much larger number than would ever succumb to the use of any currently outlawed drug. Yet we accept, as we should, that American citizens have the right to choose whether or not to smoke cigarettes.

Our politicians spend billions to sustain a system that throws hundreds of thousands of peaceful and otherwise law-abiding citizens into jails, ruins lives, and tears parents from their children. In 2000, 735,000 Americans were arrested just on marijuana charges — nearly ninety percent of them for simple possession.

A few more examples illuminate the extent of the tragedy:

- An attractive young woman named Diana Gonzales Buchanan writes from prison: "I am 30 years old and have been incarcerated since the age of 24. I am serving a 25-year sentence for 'conspiracy to possess with the intent to distribute a controlled substance'. I am one of many young individuals who have received longer and harsher sentences due to mandatory minimums and the politicians' crusades."
- Michaelene Sexton: Date of birth, 1951. Sentence: ten years for cocaine. Priors: none.
- Duane C. Edwards: Date of birth, 1969, ten years, crack cocaine, no priors.

- Brenda Pearson: Date of birth, 1953, Michigan. Sentence: 50-200 years for ten counts of delivery of cocaine (she sent small amounts to a friend). No priors.
- Eric Marsh: Date of birth, 1956, cocaine sale, no priors. Sentence: fifteen years to life.
- Monica Boguille: Date of birth, 1973. Federal sentence: ten years for crack cocaine "conspiracy." No priors.

Finally, a child sends a letter to the president, asking for amnesty for a parent: "I know what my dad did was wrong," Brandon Hogsed writes in a child's carefully drawn letters, "but do you have to take him away from me for ten years? I know from watching TV that there's killers in jail for less time than my daddy did. Please he didn't hurt anyone. Please let him come home."

A small but significant fraction of Americans will always be dependent on (or simply use) some kind of drug or other substance. We must accept this fact, do our best to help people who are addicted, and educate our children about the real dangers of drugs instead of acting as if we can eliminate this "sin" by criminalizing it and throwing users in jail.

CHAPTER FOURTEEN
Braid Hair, Break the Law

"Mama, that hurts!" Maylene said.

"Well, I guess I pulled a little too hard," said Maylene's mother, Lucille. "But if you want cornrows, they've got to be tight."

"Okay. It's okay now, Mama."

"You're real good at that," said Alexandria. She was Lucille's best friend and Maylene's godmother. "I've got at least two friends who want their hair like that, in cornrows and those perfect braids you do. Why don't you go into business?"

"I don't know. Could I charge people to braid their hair?"

"Isn't this the land of the free?" Alexandria said. "You're a good braider, and those rows are beautiful. Why not make a little money at it?"

"Well, let me try it out on your friend Berta. I know her. Then let's see."

So Lucille did Berta's hair. Alexandria and Maylene watched, and oohed and ahhed over the result. Long, tiny braids were draped in graceful swirls around Berta's head. She looked elegant. "It's wonderful!" Alexandria said.

"Do you think so?" Berta asked.

Berta showed off her braids to her friends at the university where she worked, and a lot of them wanted to know where she'd had them done.

"It's my friend Lucille," said Berta. "She's real good. Here's her phone number."

Lucille began braiding hair. One after another, Berta's and Alexandria's friends came to her. They were almost all pleased with what she did with their hair. They told her what they wanted and she did her best to provide it; braiding, locking, and weaving. They told their friends. Lucille had started a small business, and she was beginning to save some money.

Then one day Denise Roberts, one of her customers, told her that she was breaking the law.

"You have to have a cosmetology license," said Denise. "I don't know how you get one, but I told them at the salon on Twenty-second Street that you were braiding my hair, and they got pretty worked up about it. I'm sorry, I probably shouldn't have said anything. At least I didn't mention your last name or your address. But I do think you need a license."

Lucille asked around. Braiding hair for money apparently did require a license. Licensing, she discovered, meant 1,600 hours of training, including extensive training in the use of chemicals in treating hair. She didn't use chemicals, and she had no interest in them. The training would cost a minimum of $7,000. For Lucille, this was out of the question.

Lucille got out of the business. Berta and Alexandria were especially disappointed because they liked being liberated from hair straighteners and hot combs, and they enjoyed the chance to have their hair done right in the neighborhood.

What's Happening Here

When the government gets involved in matters of taste and style, its intrusion is particularly insupportable. An example: for several years New York state's cosmetology regulations kept Vidal Sassoon from doing business there. New York's state government wanted Sassoon to take an examination in finger-waving, reverse pin-curling, and thinning hair, all practices that he abhorred and that none of his decidedly up-scale clientele would dream of requesting. When Sassoon's growing reputation as a hairdresser made the regulators look increasingly ridiculous the state cosmetology board finally "updated" the test.

Today many women, including thousands of West African immigrants, learn hair braiding from friends and relatives. They seldom use chemicals. Few can afford the expense and time required to get cosmetology licenses, and many practice illegally in their homes. In 1996, California state regulators fined The Braiderie, a specialized salon in San Diego, for "aiding and abetting" unlicensed hairstyling by African immigrants. In 1998, the Ohio state Cosmetology Board defended its policy that braiding hair without a license is "a crime and should be punished by jail time."

Such policies are preposterous. They prevent decent people from making a living and prevent others from obtaining reasonably priced services. Beyond that, such regulations suppress innovation. The cosmetology courses required for licensure typically teach methods and styles that are decades behind the times. In a bureaucratized system, there is no room for invention, innovation, or change.

The political impetus for such rules is the income of those practitioners who are already licensed. Like the craft guilds of old, those who are licensed are powerfully motivated to keep out new competition, particularly competition that's likely to charge a lower price. So they appeal to the government, which, in the guise of "protecting" the public, maintains legal barriers to entry for all newcomers.

The government has no business in the hair styling business. Anyone should be allowed to cut, braid, lock, weave, wave, or otherwise fedoodle with anyone else's hair under any arrangement acceptable to the parties immediately concerned.

CHAPTER FIFTEEN
Under "Enemy" Attack

Henry Brooks had not had a drink for two and a half years. He was immensely proud of this fact, and his wife, Elaine, felt her life had been transformed. She no longer spent the evening hours wondering where her husband was or wondering if he would drink too much at a reception at the country club and get into a shouting match with one of his friends. Henry drove when they went out now, which was also a big relief for Elaine. And now in the evenings, watching television together, she could relax, knowing that a time bomb was not slowly developing in the armchair next to hers.

Henry was an avid golfer. He had continued to play golf regularly, even in his drinking years, and he was a moderately good player. One result of his passion for golf was the fact that much of the Brooks's life revolved around the West Elmira Country Club, where Elaine would share a Cobb salad and a glass of wine with two or three of her friends for Saturday lunch, waiting for Henry and his playing partners to finish their eighteen holes and join them at the Nineteenth Hole, a restaurant with a picture window that looked out on a large putting green with a "19" flag in one of the cups.

In the old days Henry had headed straight from his golf cart to the bar, where he would have a stein of dark German beer laced with bourbon. The bourbon was a secret, or had been for a good many years, between him and Luigi, the bartender. In twenty-two years of playing golf and drinking a variety of alcoholic beverages at West Elmira Country Club's several watering holes, Henry made many generous gifts to Luigi, especially at Christmas time and on Father's Day. These days, of course, Henry saw a good deal less of Luigi and had no special reason to tip him, but out of respect for times past, he still slipped Luigi something extra on special occasions.

Henry and Elaine had one child, a boy named Arlen. He was a little self-centered, as only children often are, but he seemed responsive to the disciplines of an upbringing by loving parents who tried not to let their indulgence seep over into permissiveness.

Henry had doted on Arlen from the beginning. He took on more than a father's usual share of diaper changing and night feedings, and had been pleased to do so. He had researched the purchase of toys and athletic equipment with great diligence, poring over issues of *Consumer Reports* to make sure that Arlen's ice skates, in-line skates, or lacrosse sticks were the best that money could buy.

Arlen sailed through his first two years of high school with consistently satisfactory marks, keeping out of trouble and participating actively in sports. He loved basketball, and continued to play, though it was clear by the end of his sophomore year that he would never make the first-string varsity.

When he was sixteen, Arlen began smoking cigarettes, but not in front of Henry or Elaine. Henry knew that his son was smoking behind their backs but he was not greatly perturbed by this as it seemed a pretty moderate form of adolescent rebellion. So far as Henry could see, his son had no problems with alcohol or with drugs, though everyone in the family was aware that certain elements in the high school were into these things, a few of them very deeply.

Henry and Elaine trusted Arlen; he seemed to be worthy of that trust, his rebelliousness confined mostly to surly argumentation with his mother, the cigarettes in the garage, and his refusal for two years to attend any functions at the country club, which he pronounced "unbearably square." His boycott of country club functions temporarily ended when his mother told him that Suzanne Walsh, a very attractive girl in Arlen's algebra class, was spending a fair bit of time there, particularly on the tennis courts and at the pool. "The pool's okay, I guess," Arlen allowed, and began going with his parents on warm days.

It was on August 27th, exactly two weeks after Henry's fiftieth birthday, that the phone on the nightstand between the twin beds in Henry and Elaine's bedroom jangled Henry from a very deep sleep. He picked it up.

"Yeah?"

"Henry?"

"Yeah."

"Burt Murphy. Sheriff Murphy."

"Yes, Burt. What is it? Is anyone hurt? Is Arlen okay?"

"He's okay, Henry, but he's in trouble. He's not hurt or anything. He's here. I'm holding him, and I'm going to have to hold him overnight. It's drugs."

"What!"

"I shouldn't even be calling you about this, Henry. But since we know each other, I figured you should know. That's all I can say about it."

"What's the accusation, what's the allegation?"

"I can't say anything further about it. You can come down after eight o'clock in the morning. You probably want to get Arlen a lawyer."

"Wah...?" But Burt Murphy had hung up.

Elaine was fully awake. "Arlen's in trouble. That was Sheriff Murphy. He says he's got to hold him in jail overnight. Jesus. He says it's drugs. I can't believe Arlen would be dealing or anything, impossible! Maybe some other kids he hangs out with... pot or something. Well, maybe a night in jail will be a good lesson for him. Teach him the law is serious business."

"Will he be all right? Will he be safe there?"

"Sure. He's under Burt Murphy's supervision now. We know Burt. He'll be safe. He'll be okay."

"He's a good boy, Henry. He wouldn't do anything wrong, not on purpose."

"I know it," said Henry. "They might make him do some community service."

The next morning Henry was waiting outside Sheriff Murphy's office when Murphy arrived for work. Murphy nodded a greeting. "Terrible thing, these kids. And drugs. Terrible thing Henry, I have to tell you."

"Yeah. But you know Arlen's not mixed up in any of this, Burt. He's a good kid."

"Let's go inside." Sheriff Murphy motioned Henry into a chair facing his desk. "First of all, I'd advise you to get a lawyer. Right away. This is serious business. Your son was with three other boys from high school. A packet of crack cocaine was found in the car. There were two transactions. We have a witness, an agent. Since all four boys were in the car, that's conspiracy to sell crack cocaine. There were nearly five ounces in the packet. That makes the penalty fifteen years in jail."

"You're kidding. You've got to be kidding. You know Arlen, he wouldn't sell drugs. He wouldn't even touch crack cocaine."

"Maybe not. But he had some pot, gave a joint to one of the other boys, they talked about a price. So he's in it, up to his neck."

"You can't mean you're going to charge Arlen with a serious crime? We smoked pot in Vietnam! And you *know* Arlen. You can't mean to charge him with a crime that carries a long jail term!"

"I don't make the law, Mr. Brooks, I only ...."

"'Mr. Brooks'? Why call me 'Mr. Br'...?"

"I'm telling you I don't make the law, I enforce it. The law says if your son was in a car where crack cocaine was dealt, he's part of a conspiracy to sell crack cocaine. There were over four ounces, and the punishment is fifteen years."

"You're not serious? Arlen had some pot, not crack. There weren't any weapons or anything, were there?"

"No. No weapons."

"Thank God."

"It may not make much difference. Possession of four ounces of crack cocaine with intent to sell is a more serious felony than armed robbery, or even assault with a deadly weapon. I happen to think that's not right, but it's the law."

"But you don't have to enforce laws when you feel it's wrong. There are a lot of laws you don't enforce unless there are citizen complaints, isn't that true?"

"There are some laws... and yes, citizen complaints make a difference, but the war on drugs — there's a lot of pressure on me to show we're fighting the war on drugs, doing something about the drug problem in the community, and I am here to enforce the law."

"I can't believe you're sitting there telling me that you may charge Arlen with a felony that carries a fifteen year sentence? Surely you're not telling me that?"

"I am telling you that, Henry. You should get your son a lawyer."

Things got worse. The DA put heavy pressure on Arlen to testify against his two friends. The driver of the car was a classmate of his, a boy nicknamed Beanie, who was also a junior varsity basketball player. The other one in the front seat was a senior, a boy the other three didn't know very well, and he turned out to be a snitch. The cops had arrested him on a marijuana charge a few months before, and he was trying to get a reduced sentence, though even he seemed surprised to see the crack. Leon Benning, the fourth boy, was a running back on the Elmira High School varsity football team and when he showed them the crack he had hidden in his shoe the others had been shocked.

Benning was in the deepest. The snitch testified that he had brought the cocaine to the car. He also testified about Arlen's pot. Arlen had three joints he'd gotten from another classmate, and Arlen told his father the three of them — not the snitch, who had declined — had puffed their joints and that's all that had happened in the car. Arlen also told his father and James Almore, the lawyer his father hired, that he thought Benning was probably going to sell the crack to some of the guys in the tough crowd he normally ran with. But, as James informed Henry repeatedly, the presence of crack cocaine in the car multiplied the penalties for all three of the boys to a much higher level, even though they had not used it, had not sold it, had not even possessed it. Simply being there made them part of a crack "conspiracy."

"There must be a way we can work something out," Henry said to James after their third meeting, when the facts of the case and the seriousness of the charges had sunk in.

"You would think so. You would think that a reasonable prosecutor would give Arlen a break. Or if he didn't, that a sentencing judge would see that a boy who's never been in trouble shouldn't do hard time. A judge can see how a long jail sentence would destroy a young man's life. But the war on drugs isn't like that anymore. Burt's a pretty good sheriff, but he's gotten caught up in this thing. The Sheriff Department's gotten a lot of benefit from the proceeds of property they've seized in connection with drug offenses, and he believes the community wants him to strictly enforce the drug laws. Arlen's eighteen years old, and that means he gets treated as an adult. And the judge's hands are tied. Conspiracy to sell crack cocaine, with possession of more than four ounces — just a half dozen little sugar-sized packets — carries a mandatory minimum sentence of fifteen years. The judge just isn't allowed to mitigate that minimum sentence in any way. It's not fair, but there's no way around it."

Henry had several long talks with Arlen. They discussed all possible strategies they could think of except one: Henry could not bring himself to suggest that Arlen give evidence about the other boys. Henry had served six months on active duty in Vietnam in 1969. The men in his platoon, though sometimes contemptuous of their officers, had been fiercely loyal to one another. They had been in combat seven times; two of Henry's buddies had been killed; one, his femur smashed by an enemy bullet, had lain in an open rice paddy until Henry dragged him to safety. Henry had taught Arlen that you must always be loyal to your friends, to your buddies. If anything was important in life it was that. Loyalty to your country means you go off to war when asked. Loyalty to your friends means you risk your life for them.

Henry and Elaine took out a second mortgage on their house and cashed in some of their savings to make bail for Arlen, to retain James, and meet the other expenses of their son's defense. There would be a trial. Burt Murphy had not held out enough of a compromise, short of Arlen's providing testimony against his friends, to make a plea bargain worthwhile. James urged his client with everything at his command to provide the testimony against the others that would entitle him to a reduction in sentence. But Arlen was firm. He would not betray his friends.

At one point, even his father broke down. "I know I've always taught you otherwise. But this is fifteen years, your college years, getting married. This could destroy your whole life. It kills me to say it, but maybe you should provide the testimony... I don't know, but if you provide the testimony the sentence may be reduced enough so that you'll have a life to lead after it's over." Henry stopped. He was choking on the words.

"I can't do it, Dad. You know, what about that guy you got the medal for in Vietnam, and all the ones who didn't make it? I can't do it."

Arlen refused to testify against the others.

He was convicted of conspiracy to sell crack cocaine and sentenced to fifteen years in prison.

The night after the sentencing, Elaine went to Krogers to buy some groceries. She bought spare ribs, Henry's favorite, and some fresh asparagus. As she came up the steps to their back porch and through the kitchen door, she saw Henry seated at the kitchen table. She stopped and stared at the pale glass of cola-colored liquid in her husband's hand, and the all-too-familiar slouching of his body. Tears welled in her eyes.

"You know what?" Henry said, looking up at her. He stood, unsteadily. With great care and attention he took a long, slow drink. "You know what I feel like doing? I feel like taking the flag that we always put out on holidays, taking it down to the little park in front of the Post Office and setting it on fire, and saying 'There!' *That's* what I think of your government, *that's* what I think of your..." He stopped. "Did I say 'your'? Oh God, Elaine, did I say 'your'?"

"Henry, please stop drinking. Please!"

"I'll stop when they give me my son back." He leaned his hand into the refrigerator, sliding a little magnetic dog along the surface. Then he stood straight and still. "I'll stop when I can believe in the United States of America again."

What's Happening Here

In 1997 the organization, Common Sense for Drug Policy, conducted a survey of parents whose children had been incarcerated for minor drug offenses. The purpose of the research was to find out how family members deal with the effects of the incarceration of their kids. CSDP policy analyst Paul Lewin reports:

"The respondents' experience with the judicial system leaves them feeling that their government is an agent that is causing unacceptable and unnecessary harm to their children's lives. They feel powerless to protect their children and view the long-term incarceration of their children as a huge loss to their lives.

"The perception of damaging aggression by the state coupled with their powerlessness to rescue their child gives rise to a number of emotional responses. These include anger, depression, embarrassment, silence, isolation, and fear. However, the overwhelming, unanimous emotional response is a cynicism toward the state and its institutions."

The research shows that parents of children who are given long jail sentences in such circumstances react principally by feeling that they have been victimized by the state; they come to see the government as their enemy. A few comments from parents interviewed during this study illustrate the point.

"I began to truly understand that this was not really about Sam, and it was not about fairness, and it was not about justice — it was about prosecutors trying to be able to demonstrate that they were arresting people... and Sam just happened to be caught up in that."

"If they don't cooperate and testify against the other guys, then they stand alone.... He wasn't willing to testify against anyone else. So by him doing that, they just gave him the whole nine yards — that sentence [life plus forty years for conspiracy to distribute crack cocaine]."

"Punish them, you know, but don't totally ruin them. A lot of kids are being totally ruined by the law."

The cynicism that most of the parents expressed was very deep:

"I realized that they [the prosecutors and police] had cut corners, I realized that they fudged and lied to meet their objectives."

"This entire democracy vote, and everything else, is nothing but a goddamn business. And the politicians are in the business for it, and you begin seeing what is really going on. So it's been a very enlightening experience."

"...I know the government is evil."

Lewin sums up: "This severity of the sanction[s], combined with their own treatment by police, judges, and prosecutors made [these parents]... view the state as an aggressor that was actively harming their child.... The data suggested that this cynicism was a permanent change in the respondents' lives which led them to view themselves as members of a group of people who had been harmed by their government.... The idea that a class identity may be created, especially one that forms around the idea that such people are victims of state aggression, represents a significant sociological [shift]."

The United States now has the world's highest incarceration rate, having passed Russia for that dubious honor in 2000 when the number of Americans in jail went over two million for the first time. The rate at which we were locking up our citizens in 2002 was nearly five times our own national historical norm and it continues to cost us over $40 billion per year. Approximately 450,000 of the two million plus in our jails are there for nonviolent drug offenses, many of them for mere possession. *The National Journal* estimates that, if present trends continue, one in twenty Americans will serve time in prison during his or her lifetime. If those there on drug offenses have two or three close family members who have been affected by the experience in the way the parents quoted here have been affected, then a substantial and growing percentage of our population is learning to hate our government and our police.

Chapter Sixteen
Waste Products

Paul was going to have to smuggle a toilet in from Mexico. It had been nearly impossible to get a high-flow toilet in the United States since 1999. There were a few available on the black market as a result of careful salvaging from the demolition of older buildings, but now, if you needed a high-flow toilet, smuggling from Canada or Mexico was the best alternative. It wasn't illegal to bring in a foreign toilet for your own use, but no one in the U.S. could sell you one.

There was no question that Paul and Rachel needed a high-flow toilet. The one the kids used was beyond repair and the new low-flow models, mandated by federal law to use no more than 1.6 gallons per flush, wouldn't be sufficient when the camp kids were in the house. Paul and Rachel ran a day camp for three two-week periods every summer. They had as many as fifteen kids engaged in nature walks and biology lessons, plus splashing around in their wading pool and using their bathroom. These kids used lots of toilet paper. One of their regulars, a rambunctious nine-year-old named Elise, actually brought her toilet paper with her. Her mother insisted that she was allergic to the chemicals in most brands.

Paul and Rachel's regular plumber did not want to discuss the details of obtaining a high-flow toilet. It was illegal for him to buy or sell one and, as far as contractors were concerned, there weren't any exceptions without permission. There was a long series of forms that Paul could fill out which might or might not result in official authorization for a larger-tank toilet, but the process was both lengthy and risky. If you were turned down, the subsequent installation of any illegal toilet in the house would call attention to their need for a high-flow toilet, and bring it to the attention of the toilet police, perhaps at very high levels in Washington.

Paul had remonstrated with the plumber. He told the man that his plumbing contractor had been cooperative in New York City, when he'd had a bidet installed in his apartment there. Bidets had been illegal in Manhattan for decades. But Paul and his first wife Seana lived in Manhattan and Seana wanted a bidet. The plumbers told them, sure, we just have to get the inspection done before the bidet is put in. You can *buy* bidets in Manhattan, you just can't *install* one. So, when the work was in progress Paul had stood by as the waste line for the bidet was stuffed with newspaper, a farcical camouflage of its intended use. The inspectors arrived, looked it all over, presumably took whatever bribe they were entitled to for overlooking the illegal bidet connection, and signed the necessary papers.

But at Paul and Rachel's day camp house there was no such flexibility on the matter of illegal plumbing. High-flow toilets were out and there was no plumber or contractor who was willing to provide one. The Mexican import would take two months. Meanwhile Rachel called Don's Johns and had a temporary portable latrine set up for the kids on the hillside that led down to the river. The portable johns used a lot of chemicals, which bothered Rachel, but you had to make some compromises.

What's Happening Here

In 1994 Congress passed a low-flow toilet law, mandating that all new toilets sold in the United States of America operate on 1.6 gallons of water per flush (gpf), compared with the typical 3.5 gpf previously. Even politicians seem a little embarrassed about this. Everyone seems to recognize that it is idiotic for the federal government to be in the business of mandating toilet design. Jokes abound. "Homeowners all across America... are frustrated to tears with this kind of government meddling. So we're going to flush them out," remarked House Majority Leader Richard K. Armey (R-Tex) in 1999.

The amount of water "saved" by this pointless law is trivial. All of America could go back to using outhouses tomorrow and it would have little impact on water consumption. The real water waste is in the subsidized irrigation of crops in nineteen Western states, where water is sloshed around on a Brobdingnagian scale, consuming more than eighty percent of our national water supply. But that doesn't much interest the toilet police, for whom saving water isn't really the point.

Instead, the government, spurred on by a handful of enviro-zealots who find it more satisfying to control other people's lives than to address serious issues of water conservation, is following its normal busybody instincts, forcing us to do its bidding in our bathrooms. The same law, by the way, mandates low-flow shower heads, so it is getting harder and harder to have a satisfying shower. One response has been the installation of second "body" showerheads, thus confounding the purpose of the law by doubling the (otherwise reduced) flow of water.

Americans prefer to laugh about this kind of petty-seeming paternalism because the inconvenience is increasingly minor. But what conceivable business has the government in our toilets anyway? Is it really so funny that the government is creeping into our bathrooms, into our bathtubs, into our very commodes?

CHAPTER SEVENTEEN
Yes, the State Can Take Your Home

Henriette Johanssen and her husband, Per, lived in a small two-bedroom cottage overlooking tiny Lake Matatopa in the upper Midwest. Per had worked as an auditor and accountant for the firm of Touche Ross and he and Henriette had become summer regulars at Matatopa's Green Cove cabins, where they reserved, when they could, a favorite cabin near a point that defined the southern end of the cove. When it came time to retire, the Johanssens were able to buy a lot that overlooked "their" cove from the opposite side of the lake.

Henriette and Per paid a great deal of attention to constructing their home. Per worked side by side with the contractor building the house, and had sealed a lock of Henriette's hair and a short note he had composed (and did not show to anyone else), addressed to "the people of the twenty-third century," in a triple-thick plastic envelope, which he had put in the hollow part of one of the cinder blocks in the foundation; he had mortared that block in himself.

Per had also done much of the finishing work — the wainscoting, the beveled paneling around the windows and a lot of the cabinetwork. The two central cabinets in the kitchen were fronted by doors that depicted well-known Swedish historical legends. The door panels had been carved in Sweden; Henriette and Per had brought them back from a trip to what they still called "the home country," even though they themselves were second-generation Americans.

Henriette made the curtains and slipcovers for much of their furniture. She had crocheted the tiny curtains that hung in the half bathroom off the short front hallway.

In the main bathroom, the neat, white tile work depicted bright scenes of birches and pine trees in a repeated pattern around the tub and behind both sinks. The birches and pines were interrupted over the left-hand sink for the word "Henriette" in old-fashioned script; over the other sink, the interruption was much shorter for "Per."

Three weeks after the house was completed and the contractor was finally gone, the grass seed on the new lawn began to sprout with pale green shoots. The house was theirs, except for the mortgage, of course. Per went to work in his basement shop with a router on an oblong piece of pine, bordered by bark. When he had finished burning the letters into the wood he gave the sign three coats of varnish, rubbed it down with extra-fine steel wool, and hung it from a post right in front of the house. The sign read: "Dis-L-Doo." Two weeks later he hung a similarly routered sign just beneath "Dis-L-Doo" which said "The Johanssens."

Much of the Johanssens' life in retirement revolved around their home. Except in the sometimes bitter days of winter, Per spent two or three hours a day working around the house, touching up the exterior white paint or the dark green painted shutters. He cleaned the gutters, trimmed, fixed, and seeded the lawn, repaired worn spots on the garage roof, fixed minor plumbing problems, and continually added little touches like the graveled circle in the middle of the lawn where a cement cherub held a basin of water in which birds routinely came to bathe.

During growing season, Henriette tended a dozen rose-bushes. She also planted careful straight rows of impatiens, zinnias, and nasturtiums, which grew in box-like formation along the path leading from the "Dis-L-Doo" sign up to the front door. And she liked to oil and polish the Brazilian cher-rywood table that was the centerpiece of their dining area.

The Johanssens' daughter Sonia was married and lived in Minneapolis. Sonia was a part-time stockbroker at Dain Bosworth, and her husband, Paul, managed a hardware store. The year that Sonia had her first child, a baby girl, Per and Henriette celebrated ten years in their new home.

Henriette and Per looked forward to visits by Sonia and her family, especially on Thanksgiving. The most recent Thanksgiving celebration had gone well. Henriette's turkey had been wonderfully brown and tender, the cranberry sauce, made to the "Stanberg" recipe she'd heard over the radio (cranberries, horseradish, chopped onions, sugar and sour cream), had been a big hit, and her chocolate meringue pie was superb. Even the baby seemed to enjoy herself.

Once Sonia, Paul, and the baby had left, it took Henriette and Per two days to bring the house back to what they con-sidered the normal standard of cleanliness and order. Two days after that, the doorbell rang and they opened the door to find a policeman standing on the front porch.

"Yes sir?" Henriette said to the uniformed officer.

"I'm sorry, ma'am. I'm here to inform you that a complaint has been filed to forfeit your house to the state. Your house has been the scene of a crime. It is therefore forfeitable. You have ten days to respond and ask for a hearing, or the court will enter a default judgment, empowering us to confiscate your house and the property it's on. You must file any reply within ten days at Superior Court."

He handed her a sheaf of papers.

Stunned, Henriette stared at him in silence, and after a moment he turned to go. "What are you talking about?" she asked.

"I'm sorry, ma'am. Your house has been the scene of a crime on several occasions, so it's forfeitable. We can confiscate it because it has facilitated the crime. It's the law."

"What crime? We've never done anything…."

"I'm not supposed to go into it, but we've been investigating marijuana use and selling in the area. Several teenagers have admitted to smoking marijuana in your basement last Tuesday. We pulled them in the next day for reckless driving and two of them agreed to cooperate on the marijuana case. There's even been some buying and selling of marijuana on these premises. So we're moving to confiscate the house. I'm sorry."

"I don't understand."

"Ma'am, it's all there in the papers. We're confiscating your house. You can file a response, but you have to do it within ten days. It probably won't work — we have two confessions to a crime on the premises. That means we can take it. The proceeds will be used for law enforcement."

"I don't understand, I still don't understand. We haven't done anything! Whoever smoked marijuana in our basement may have done something wrong, but we haven't done anything wrong and it's our house. What are you talking about? Who smoked marijuana here? Why aren't you arresting them? How can you possibly punish Per and me? We've done nothing. I mean, we have absolutely done nothing wrong. We have no interest in smoking marijuana or anything like that. How can you..."

"Ma'am. You don't have to do anything wrong. You are not being punished. Some teenagers have been using your basement. Do you keep it locked?"

"Usually. Sometimes Per leaves it unlocked so Ben Pedersen next door can use the workbench. There's nothing down there to steal."

"Well, if you left it unlocked you haven't done enough to prevent this crime, so your house is forfeitable. It's called an 'in-rem' proceeding. You can think of it like the house committed the crime, so we're confiscating the house. We're not accusing you of anything personally."

"You're not accusing us, you're just fining us $225,000, our life savings, our home, the main thing that matters to us. You're taking it away from us. That's not punishing *us*?"

"I'm sorry, Ma'am. That's the law."

Henriette and Per replied within the ten-day limit, a frantic hardship in itself, but the judge, though she was sympathetic, said her hands were tied. The police had solid confessions to a crime on the premises; it was a drug crime; the house was forfeitable. It didn't matter who owned it or what their own criminal history or lack of it was. In an "in-rem" proceeding, these things didn't make any difference. The judge was sorry, she said, but the police had a right to their property. They would have to vacate in twenty days.

Still disbelieving, Henriette stuttered, "You mean you're going to take away our house because two teenagers we don't even know say they were trespassing on our property without our knowledge and smoked marijuana in our basement? You're going to destroy our lives because of what some strangers have done? I can't believe it. This is the United States of America! I'm an American citizen. My husband and I are second-generation immigrants from Sweden. We thought we could live here in freedom, without the police marching in in the middle of the night to terrorize and destroy. What has this country come to?"

"I'm sorry, Mrs. Johanssen," the judge said. "The law is clear. A crime was committed in your house, and the house is forfeitable under this state's drug laws. The legislature did not provide an innocent owner defense, and *Bennis v. Michigan* says that you do not have a constitutional right to one. So there's nothing I can do. I'm truly sorry."

The state claimed the house and boarded it up, posting a large sign outside that said it had been the subject of a forfeiture as a crime scene. Henriette and Per scraped together just enough money to buy a small mobile home which they lined up with several dozen others in a park called "Arcadia" on the edge of town. There was room for a rose bush and three zinnia plants. The dining table was plywood, but serviceable. On weekends in the summer they often went to the public beach on Lake Matatopa.

Two years after they moved into the trailer, Henriette had to be taken to the hospital. It was a stroke, or maybe a heart attack, or perhaps a broken heart. Despite extraordinary efforts to save her, she died within five days. Per died two months later.

What's Happening Here

Hundreds of civil asset forfeiture cases similar to the Johanssens' are part of the "War on Drugs." Homes, automobiles, aircraft, boats, cash, and other property have been seized by police from innocent owners.

Donald Scott, the sixty-one-year-old owner of a California ranch, was shot and killed in his home in 1992 during a police raid propelled by the desire to seize his 200-acre ranch. The police claimed that marijuana was being grown on the premises, an allegation that proved to be false.

In 1989 the U.S. Customs Service seized and "inspected" Craig Klein's new $24,000 sailboat in what turned out to be a fruitless drug search; the boat was damaged beyond repair, but the Customs Service refused to compensate Klein, who was forced to sell it for scrap.

In 1991, Willie Jones, the owner of a landscaping service, had $9,600 in cash seized by the Drug Enforcement Agency, which suspected that anyone carrying so much cash (Jones was planning to use cash to purchase plants and shrubbery from growers in Houston) must be dealing in drugs. No charges were ever brought against him, but the government kept his money for more than two years, requiring him to incur substantial legal costs to get it back.

In one case a woman actually had her car confiscated by the police because her estranged husband was convicted of engaging in "lascivious conduct" in it with a prostitute.

And, as noted in chapter six, a woman's home in Washington, D.C., was trashed because, unknown to her, drugs had been sold on the front porch.

The idea that the government is empowered to seize property that has been involved in a crime without considering the hardship that's inflicted upon owners dates back to an ancient past in which people believed in the inherent ability of inanimate objects to cause harm. In the fifteenth century, for example, slates falling from roofs and injuring passersby were ceremoniously carried to county borderlines and "cast out" as punishment for their offenses.

Today our laws still reflect this bizarre concept, and related laws reflect the powerful motivation of police and other law enforcement authorities who are entitled, under most forfeiture legislation, to keep the proceeds of the sale of forfeited property. Had the California police succeeded in seizing Donald Scott's 200-acre ranch, for example, they would have sold it after seizure, and several million dollars would have flowed into the coffers of local law enforcement. At the very least, this is an egregious conflict of interest.

Civil asset forfeiture tears the fabric of the Constitution's Fourth Amendment which states that "The right of people to be secure in their persons, houses, papers, and effects, against unreasonable searches and seizures, shall not be violated[.]" The Supreme Court permits these forfeiture cases, which would otherwise violate the Constitution, because they are brought under the provisions of civil law; criminal law provides citizens much greater protections. But most of the people who have lost their property in these civil cases have never been threatened with criminal prosecution; rather, in a process almost literally akin to stealing, the police seize their property because the property itself is associated with the commission of a crime. Further, as in the cases of Craig Klein and Willie Jones, property is often seized when there has been no crime committed at all.

The situation has gotten so far out of hand that conservative U.S. Congressman Henry Hyde asked, in 1995, whether these systematic abuses of our rights may be leading us toward "an American police state." Hyde characterized many police as "addicted to forfeiture.... Law enforcement has become hooked on forfeiture as surely as the junkie nodding on the corner is hooked on drugs — the addiction of the latter has begotten the addiction of the former. They both must have their fix." Hyde cites an outraged Philadelphia city council member who noted that "while Philadelphia police had $4 million in available forfeiture funds to spend on air conditioning police offices, car washes, emergency postage, office supplies, and fringe benefits, the city's chemical lab where drugs are analyzed, had a backlog of more than 3,000 cases, forcing defendants to wait months longer for trial — many in jail unable to afford bail."

Happily, Hyde and his Democratic colleague on the House Judiciary Committee, John Conyers, succeeded in amending the Federal forfeiture laws in 2000. While the federal government must now follow more stringent rules before they can seize your property, they can still do it. And the forfeiture laws of most states are as bad as ever.

CHAPTER EIGHTEEN

The Heavy Hand of the State: A Sampler

The stories and essays in this book cover laws that inhibit the operation of small businesses; prevent citizens from making their own automobiles safer; deprive Americans of their homes, property, and liberty without justification; undermine the "Great Writ" of habeas corpus; prevent legitimate economic activity; enervate charities; attempt to govern private sexual behavior; undermine (unintentionally) the happiness and well-being of lower-income Americans; and regulate pornography, marijuana, and toilets. Believe it or not, this is only a small sample. A few others are:

- Most forms of gambling are illegal in all states but Nevada. This includes the Friday night poker game in your home and the football pool in your office.
- Wine makers cannot cite the benefits of their product on the labels of their product, even though those benefits have been well established.
- The number of laws and regulations governing what you can do to your house, how far it must be from your neighbor's garage, what the pitch of your roof must be, whether or not you can (or must) have front windows, and similar matters, is a list so long, containing so many

details about how we are expected to live, that it could fill an entire library. These regulations also provide lots of opportunities for corruption. A friend of mine, whose house is half a mile from his nearest neighbor, was told by a building inspector that he would have to rip recently installed shingles off the little roof over the entranceway to his house and replace them with another material because the four-by-four-foot piece of roof did not have sufficient pitch for shingles, according to the "Code." Heated words were exchanged. The matter was resolved only after the inspector had a chat with my friend's building contractor in private. The shingles stayed.

- In Texas the legislature made it illegal in 1999 to get extra pairs of prescription glasses if the prescription is more than a year old. This means that the eye technicians in Texas can cadge an extra $100 or so from hundreds of thousands of Texas citizens who have to get their eyes reexamined every year just to get the same glasses they've used all their lives. Who do you suppose lobbied for that one?

- In St. John's County, Florida, the revealing of any part of the buttocks is outlawed on public beaches. The ordinance takes 350 words to define buttocks ("The area at the rear of the human body... which lies between two [lines], the top such line being one half inch below the top of the vertical cleavage of the nates... and the bottom such line being one half inch above the lowest point of the curvature of the fleshy protuberance (sometimes referred to as the gluteal fold) and between two imaginary straight lines..." and so on).

- Federal law requires that dairy farmers get artificially high prices for their milk, based on a formula involving the distance of the producer from Eau Claire, Wisconsin.

Consumers outside of Wisconsin pay more for their milk as a result.

- In Chincoteague, Virginia, two ladies who sell fresh vegetables to the tourists were required to build a cement curb in front of their vegetable stand. The curb impedes access and makes driving into or parking near the stand more difficult and serves absolutely no useful purpose.

- Laws governing the labeling of products have become so absurd that few Americans bother to read the warnings on product labels anymore. A package of sleeping aids carried the phrase "Warning — may cause drowsiness." The owners of strollers are admonished to "remove child before folding." A string of Christmas lights is "For indoor or outdoor use only."

- Until 2001 it was illegal to tell people's fortunes or read their palms for money in sixty-one of North Carolina's 100 counties (and the law, though declared unconstitutional by one of North Carolina's superior courts, is still on the books).

- Child labor laws prevent perfectly healthy youngsters from doing work they would be glad to do, even under the supervision of family members. Sorry.

- Three states prohibit (and, in 2002, the matter was on appeal in a fourth state) the sale of objects "intended primarily for the stimulation of the human genitals."

The list goes on and on. State and federal lawmakers seem utterly unable to stop themselves from passing law after law, regulation after regulation, micromanaging our lives in ways that not only do not work, but usually backfire. "Why doesn't everybody leave everybody else the hell alone?" Jimmy Durante once asked. Why indeed? But once part of government, people develop an uncontrollable urge to exercise power over others, like former Secretary of State Madeleine Albright, who once asked rhetorically "What's the

point of having this superb military... if we can't use it?"
Government officials seem impelled by an inner force to try
to control our lives. All of us must resist this trend, or government creep will eventually, gradually, overwhelm us.

CHAPTER NINETEEN
Five Simple Rules for Dealing With the Government

1. Assert your rights. Too many Americans, confronted by the police or other law enforcement authorities, readily grant permission for searches of their homes, persons, or cars. Unless the police have a warrant, you can resist this. You, your car, and your home may not be searched without a warrant or, at the very least, what the law calls "probable cause," which means that the police must have a serious reason to believe that there is contraband or other proof of illegal activity for them to justify the search.

Be polite, and be cooperative, but when asked "You don't mind if we look through your car then, do you?" just say politely, "I'm not giving my permission for that." Your refusal will annoy some law enforcement authorities, and they may find ways of detaining you to punish you for asserting your rights, but you should do it anyway.

If all Americans drew the line on these searches, there would be far fewer of them and our freedom from unjustified searches and seizures would be greatly enhanced, as the Fourth Amendment to the Constitution of the United States was meant to assure.

2. Obey the laws that you have to obey, and that you should obey. This applies particularly to nasty things like income tax and the grey zones of corporate behavior where it is easy to cheat. Don't do it. If you want to flout the tax laws, do so openly and be prepared to accept the consequences.

Our income tax laws are a monumental mess, and taxes on income, starting with the Social Security tax, are inexcusably regressive, excessive for most taxpayers, and arranged to govern our financial behavior in foolish and dysfunctional ways. We should have a flat tax with simple, no-exceptions rules. But in the meantime, surreptitious failure to pay what the law requires is the kind of disregard for the law that doesn't work, because it is invariably seen as selfish. In addition, if you cheat you will always be defensive with the government because you have something to hide, and will you be afraid to assert your rights.

3. Cheerfully disobey those laws that are silly or dysfunctional if the odds are in your favor and your behavior does not harm anyone. Americans routinely ignore laws governing private sexual behavior, from sodomy to fornication to adultery, and if your relationships are respectful, a violation of such laws is most unlikely to cause you any trouble. Same for gambling, if done in private. I've never heard of anyone getting busted for taking part in the office football pool, though this is a serious crime in most states, especially for those who keep track of the pool participants ("possession of gambling records").

The drug laws are trickier. Millions of healthy, industrious Americans use various forms of illegal substances from time to time and are careful not to get caught. No harm done, in most cases. But do not get hooked on anything addictive, such as heroin or nicotine.

I also wouldn't worry very much about violating the low-flow toilet laws or the minimum wage laws if you and the babysitter next door can agree on something that's fair. On the other hand, if you have any intention of entering public life, it's probably wise to pay the withholding taxes for the cleaning lady because background checks seem routinely to include such matters.

4. Make your voice heard. It's old advice but our elected representatives do read their mail, or at least count it. If letters and phone calls and e-mails keep coming in, pointing out the dangers of government excesses and how the rights of citizens are being violated through such things as asset forfeiture laws, it can make a difference.

A useful angle here is to ask both conservatives and liberals to be true to their credos. Conservative politicians, exemplified for many years by North Carolina's Jesse Helms, are ferociously proud of "keeping the government off our backs." Reminding such people that it would be nice to have the government out of our sex lives (pornography, sodomy) can be an effective argument. Similarly, liberals who want to tax and regulate private commercial enterprises into the ground should be reminded that classic liberalism means laissez-faire, free-market economics.

5. Talk this up. We all have discussions and other kinds of conversations with friends and acquaintances. Remind people that government creep endangers their rights and liberties. Remind people that, as Thomas Jefferson put it, "The natural progress of things is for liberty to yield and government to gain ground." We demand things from the government, so the government grows. Congressional representatives are rewarded when they bring home the bacon (or the pork), so government programs keep spiraling upwards, along with the taxes to support them. With this power comes the urge to control us, and that deadly combination is government creep.

Most of all, remind people that these things are going on now, that they happen to middle-class Americans as well as to poor Americans (though that would be bad enough), and that the process is building a mountain of programs, taxes, and special-interest payments that more and more threaten our status as free, independent, and responsible human beings.

CHAPTER TWENTY
Test Yourself on Statutes

Listed below are a dozen laws or regulations. Nine are real; three are made up. See if you can tell which is which. Answers and explanations are given following the list.

1. It is illegal for fishing lodges in Alaska to serve fresh salmon to their guests.

2. The city of Missoula, Montana, has outlawed the wearing of perfume in city buildings.

3. In Orinda, California, it is illegal to go horseback riding on Sundays, except on federal property.

4. Crazy Horse Malt Liquor was effectively outlawed by an act of the U.S. Congress in 1992.

5. In the District of Columbia, liquor stores can sell miniature bottles only in batches of six.

6. In Albany, New York, it is unlawful to wear cowboy boots with visible spurs in public.

7. In Los Angeles the law requires that every house must have a built-in stove.

8.   It is illegal to sell bird food in the U.S. if it contains hemp seed, even if the seed contains no measurable trace of THC (the active ingredient in marijuana).

9.   IN VINO and BUBBLY are forbidden as personalized license plates in Oregon; WACKER and BARE IT are allowed.

10. Homeowners in Los Angeles are required to construct a minimum of two parking spaces on their property even if they own only one car. Both spaces must be covered by a permanent roof.

11. In Ishpeming, Michigan, you may not drive a car that is painted both blue and "bright yellow."

12. In District C of the Los Angeles school system, high school students may not participate in graduation ceremonies unless they agree to go on to higher education or the military.

Answers/Explanations

1.   This one is real. For some reason the state of Alaska, free-wheeling as it is in many other respects, just can't bring itself to permit fishing lodges to serve fresh fish to their paying guests. It seems that any food served to clients must be "processed" through an approved system and, of course, taxed by the state. Those nice fresh salmon, which the fishing guides could (and frequently do) catch right out in the river in front of the lodge, can't be included in the menu. This can't be an issue of safety because the state permits donations of up to 500 pounds of unprocessed fresh fish to humanitarian organizations for the needy. This one is sheer busybodyness.

2. True. Perhaps some of those rough-and-tumble west-erners in the Big Sky State are supersensitive.

3. Made up. I only hope the authorities in Orinda don't read this and pass an ordinance making it real.

4. True, true, true. A huge hullabaloo was created when this beverage was introduced. Indian tribes were out-raged. Congress tried to pass a law that would make it illegal to name alcoholic beverages after dead people but that was derailed when someone pointed out that it would take Samuel Adams beer off the market. Still, Crazy Horse was too much freedom for our legislators. The brand was killed.

5. True. A little sign up on a shelf in the liquor store I oc-casionally frequent on L Street in downtown D.C. an-nounces this bizarre regulation. Attempts to get some clarification from the city as to the reasoning behind it brought perplexing responses. One official said "It must be too easy to steal." One hypothesis is that the city doesn't want the "wrong" people to buy very small quantities of liquor, but then why can liquor stores sell half pints for far less than the price of six miniatures? Go figure.

6. Made up.

7. Absolutely true. Every residence must have a "kitchen" and the definition of a kitchen is a stove with a dedi-cated electrical or gas line. If you want to call in pizza every night you still have to be prepared to cook in an emergency.

8. All too true. Because of the federal government's al-most zany obsession with marijuana, hemp, which has several of marijuana's physical characteristics, can't be

grown in the United States except under absurdly restrictive conditions. (It's legal in most other countries and a very useful product.) To be certain that the marijuana police don't get fooled by close approximations, all products containing hemp seed — if intended for ingestion by man or beast — are illegal here.

9. True. Michael P. Higgins reported in the *Ashland* [Oregon] *Daily Tidings* that the state won't let him put any slogan on his license plate that refers to an alcoholic beverage.

10. True, although no one knows why. Code regulations require two covered parking spaces for every home that's built in LA. More silly meddling.

11. This one's fictitious.

12. True. You can graduate, but you can't take part in the ceremony unless you promise the authorities that you're going on to college, trade school, an internship, or the military.

Sources

Chapter One

Tax notes: A.M. Dolinsky, CPA, personal communication, October 19, 2002.

GNP data: *The Economist*: *Pocket World in Figures*, 2002 Edition, Profile Books, Ltd., London, 2001.

Milton Friedman: "Mr. Market/A Nobelist views today's Fed, currencies, Social Security regulations," Interview, *Barron's*, August 24, 1998.

Chapter Two

Higgs: "Permanent Emergencies and Constitutional Rights," *The Lighthouse* (e-mail newsletter), Independent Institute, July 29, 2002.

Levy: "Judge Cancels Hearing for Prisoner Classified As 'Enemy Combatant,' " *Cato Daily Dispatch*, The Cato Institute, August 8, 2002.

Stuart Taylor, Jr., "Let's Not Allow a Fiat To Undermine The Bill Of Rights," *National Journal*, July 20, 2002, p. 2143.

"USA Patriot Act Boosts Government Power While Cutting Back on Traditional Checks and Balances," *An ACLU Leg-*

islative Analysis, American Civil Liberties Union Freedom Network, Fall 2002.

"Court Backs Closings of Detainees' Hearings," *Washington Post*, October 9, 2002, p. A1.

"FBI Given More Latitude/New Surveillance Rules Remove Evidence Hurdle," *Washington Post*, May 30, 2002.

"Under Fire, Justice Sinks TIPS Program," *Washington Post*, August 10, 2002.

Chapter Three

Sturges: "Photo book case still awaits trial after a year," *Birmingham News*, February 14, 1999; The Media Coalition Inc, *Summary of Outstanding Litigation*, October 4, 2002.

Sims: "Policing Photos," *Philadelphia Inquirer*, January 4, 1991.

Tin Drum: "Seizure of 1979 Art Film Draws Fire/Oklahoma Police Raids to Confiscate 'Tin Drum' Raise Privacy Issues," *Washington Post*, June 30, 1997.

"Suffer little children/Americans' overprotection of children against pedophilia." *The Economist*. September 23, 1995. p. 24.

Knox case: Anthony Lewis, "Anti-Porn zealotry outstrips common sense," *The News & Observer* (Raleigh, NC), November 30, 1993, op-ed page.

Senator Arnold: "This dog won't hunt," editorial, *The Denver Post*, February 2, 1998, p. 6B.

Chapter Four

Murray: Charles Murray, *In Pursuit of Happiness and Good Government*, ICS Press, San Francisco, 1994, p. 119.

Chapter Five

Tales of the City: Virginia Postrel, "Who Needs it?," *Forbes*, August 10, 1998. p. 123.

Lancet quote: Lynn Zimmer and John P. Morgan, *Marijuana Myths/Marijuana Facts*, Lindesmith Center, 1997, p. 6.

Chapter Six
"Bronx Man Recounts Abuse by Police in Mistaken Raid," *New York Times*, March 4, 1998.
Georgia Case: *Playboy*, February, 1990, p. 44.
"Adultery as a Crime: Old Laws Dusted Off in a Wisconsin Case, " *New York Times*, April 30, 1990, p. A1.

Chapter Seven
Freedom Cabs; Connell; "muffin lady": Clint Bolick, *Transformation*, ICS Press, 1998, pp. 80, 177-178.

Chapter Eight
Randy Fitzgerald, "Sugar's Sweet Deal," *Reader's Digest*, February, 1998, p. 91.
Tom Weiner, "It's Raining Farm Subsidies," *New York Times*, August 8, 1999, Sec. 4, p. 16.
"No More Welfare for Millionaires," *The Washington Times*, August 9, 1999, p. B5.
Farm bill: Robert J. Samuelson, "Harvesting Votes," *Washington Post*, May 8, 2002, op.ed.
"Lawmakers ditch free-market tack," *Chicago Tribune*, April 27, 2002.

Chapter Nine
Michael Kelly, "Mother of a Reinvention," *Washington Post*, June 3, 1998, op-ed.

Chapter Ten
"Adultery as a Crime," *New York Times*, April 30, 1990, *op. cit.*
R. Posner and K. Silbaugh, *A Guide To America's Sex Laws*, The University of Chicago Press, 1996, p.103.

Government Creep
What the Government is Doing That You Don't Know About
158

"Four Arrests for Adultery Raise Legal, Privacy Issues in Connecticut," *Boston Globe*, September 9, 1990.

Chapter Twelve
ADA: "Standard Accommodations: The road to universal disability," *Reason*, February 1999, p. 60
"Flab and the EEOC," *Forbes*, August 23, 1999, p. 64.

Chapter Thirteen
Young: Families Against Mandatory Minimums (F.A.M.M.), FAMM-gram, September-December, 1998.
VanWinkle: *New York Times*, February 28, 1999, p. 20.
Barkin: F.A.M.M., *op. cit.,* p. 5.
Marijuana arrests: National Organization for the Reform of Marijuana Laws (NORML), personal communication, October 17, 2002.

Chapter Fourteen
Sassoon; Braiderie: Virginia Postrel, *The Future and Its Enemies*, The Free Press, 1998, pp. 114, 115.
Ohio hair braiding: "Liberty & Law," (newsletter), *Institute for Justice,* December, 1998, p. 7.

Chapter Fifteen
"Mandatory Minimums and Parental Attitudes: The Effects of Lengthy Incarceration on Parents of Non-Violent Offenders." *12th International Conference/1999 Policy Manual*, Drug Policy Foundation, p. 61.
"America, All Locked Up," *National Journal*, August 15, 1998, p. 1906.

Chapter Sixteen
Water use: Jerry Taylor, "No Water? Blame the government," *The Washington Times*, August 17, 1999, op-ed.

Chapter Seventeen

Donald Scott; 'addicted to forfeiture': Henry Hyde, *Forfeiting Our Property Rights*, Cato Institute, 1995, pp. 14, 53.

Willy Jones: Statement of Nadine Strossen, President of The American Civil Liberties Union, before the Committee on the Judiciary of the U.S. House of Representatives, June 11, 1997.

Chapter Eighteen

Texas eyeglasses: Molly Ivins, "Envision the power of politics," *The News & Observer*, (Raleigh, NC), September 30, 1999, op-ed.

Buttocks: St. Johns County Public Nudity Ordinance (Ordinance 92-12, Section 6, paragraph 3 (c)).

Eau Clair, Wisconsin: Ron Kind, "Michigan Lobsters," *Washington Post*, September 22, 1999, p. A33.

N.C. palm reading: personal communication, Seth Jaffee, NCCLU, October 18, 2002.

Vibrators: J.M. Carpenter, Jenner & Block, personal communication, October 18, 2002.

M. Albright quote: "The World; The Powell Doctrine Is Looking Pretty Good Again," *New York Times,* April 4, 1999.

Chapter Twenty

Missoula Perfume: "A Lack of Common Scents," *Trout Wrapper*, (Belgrade, MT), July 15, 1999, p. 9

Crazy Horse: James Bovard, "The Second Murder of Crazy Horse," *Wall Street Journal*, September 19, 1992, p. A16.

Hemp seed: J.M. Carpenter, Jenner & Block, personal communication, October 18, 2002.

IN VINO: "What About my free Speech?" Michael P. Higgins, *Ashland Area Daily*, February 9, 2000.

District C, L.A.: John Leo, "Bombarded by bans," *U.S. News & World Report*, October 21, 2002, p. 12.

YOU WILL ALSO WANT TO READ:

☐ **64266 DEEP INSIDE THE UNDERGROUND ECONOMY, How Millions of Americans are Practicing Free Enterprise in an Unfree Society, by Adam Cash.** Are you fed up with giving so much of your hard earned cash to the government then watching it get spent on ridiculous pork barrel special interest projects? Would you like to hold on to more of your money for your own special interest projects? The underground economy continues to grow in spite of the ever-widening attempt by the administration to regulate and tax everything we do. Millions of Americans are practicing free enterprise in today's increasingly unfree society. You, too, can beat the system and operate your business tax free as a "guerrilla capitalist." This book shows you the ropes and how to get started. *2003, 8½ x 11, 240 pp, soft cover.* **$24.95.**

☐ **25098 GUNS SAVE LIVES, True Stories of Americans Defending Their Lives With Firearms, by Robert A. Waters.** *Guns Save Lives* is filled with true stories of Americans who altered the course of their lives and others by their use of firearms. The anti-gun lobbyists continue to harp on violence in our society being the fault of guns. Robert Waters gives us the other side of citizen defenders in this country. Those ordinary Americans who have successfully defended their lives, their families and their homes, and, in doing so, proved that our founding fathers knew what they were doing when they gave us the right to bear arms. *2002, 5½ x 8½, 184 pp, photographs, soft cover.* **$15.95.**

We offer the very finest in controversial and unusual books — A complete catalog is sent **FREE** *with every book order. If you would like to order the catalog separately, please see our ad on the next page.*

GC3

LOOMPANICS UNLIMITED
PO BOX 1197
PORT TOWNSEND, WA 98368

Please send me the books I have checked above. I am enclosing $ _____ which includes $6.25 for shipping and handling of orders up to $25.00. Add $1.00 for each additional $25.00 ordered. *Washington residents please include 8.29% for sales tax.*

NAME _____

ADDRESS _____

CITY/STATE/ZIP _____

We accept Visa, Discover, and MasterCard. To place a credit card order *only,* call 1-800-380-2230, 24 hours a day, 7 days a week.
Check out our Web site: www.loompanics.com